C# Programming

I0011505

Troy Dimes

All rights Reserved. No part of this publication or the information in it may be quoted from or reproduced in any form by means such as printing, scanning, photocopying or otherwise without prior written permission of the copyright holder.

Disclaimer and Terms of Use: Effort has been made to ensure that the information in this book is accurate and complete, however, the author and the publisher do not warrant the accuracy of the information, text and graphics contained within the book due to the rapidly changing nature of science, research, known and unknown facts and internet. The Author and the publisher do not hold any responsibility for errors, omissions or contrary interpretation of the subject matter herein. This book is presented solely for motivational and informational purposes only.

Contents

Introduction

As a thank you for reading *C# Programming*, I would like to give a free copy of *7 Little-Known C# Programming Tricks*.

To download your copy visit:
http://www.linuxtrainingacademy.com/7-tricks

Chapter 1: Creating Your First C# Program

C# is Microsoft's premier programming language and is an integral part of the Microsoft .NET framework. C# is a completely object oriented and type safe language. If you are looking forward to developing applications with Microsoft's programming technologies, C# is the best place to start. C# is currently being used for developing ASP.NET web applications, Windows forms, and WPF based desktop applications. With the advent of smart phones, C# is also used for Windows phone apps development and Android application development.

This book presents a basic overview of the core features of C# language. After reading this book you will be able to jump in to Microsoft's advanced programming technologies, such as ASP.NET, WCF, WPF, and Windows phone. The first chapter of this book explains how to install the IDE, integrated development environment, and how to create your first C# application.

Contents

1- Installing the IDE

The best software for developing C# applications is, without any doubt, Microsoft's Visual Studio integrated environment. It contains everything it takes to build professional C# applications. However, the full edition of Visual Studio is commercial. In this book, we are going to develop C# applications without spending a cent. To do this, we are going to download a trimmed-down version of Visual Studio, which is totally free. This software has more than enough features and functionality for developing basic C# applications. Follow these steps to download the software:

- Go to the following link: http://www.visualstudio.com/en-us/products/visual-studio-express-vs.aspx

- Scroll down the page and find the link for "Express 2013 for Windows Desktop". Click "Download" to download the installation file. This is shown in the following figure:

Fig 1.0

- The page that appears will ask you to login with your "Windows Live ID" or a "Microsoft Account." If you don't have one, sign up on that page.

- Once you create your ID and provide details such as your full name and country, you will be presented with a couple of versions of VS 2013 Express to download. Choose the latest version for the Windows Desktop. In this example we will be downloading "Express 2013 for Windows Desktop." This is shown in following figure:

Fig 1.1

- This will download the installation exe for "Visual Studio Express 2013 for Windows Desktop." The name of the download file will be "wdexpress_full.exe".

- Open the downloaded file. The installation wizard appears. Agree to license terms and privacy policy and click the

"Install" button at the bottom. This is shown in the following figure.

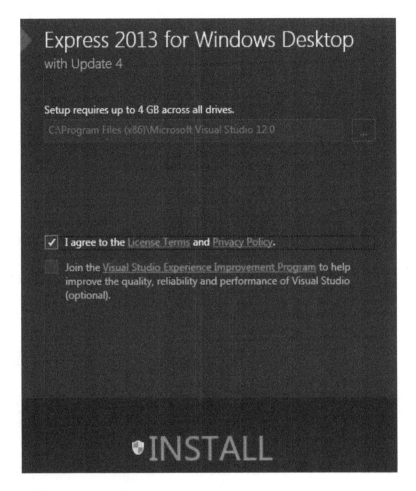

Fig 1.2

And that's it. The wizard will download the required C# components for developing web applications. You just have to keep clicking the "Next" button in the installer.

2- Creating and Running the First Application

To create your first C# application, open "Visual Studio 2013 Express," which you downloaded in the last section. Follow these steps:

- Open File => New => Project from the menu bar as shown in the following figure:

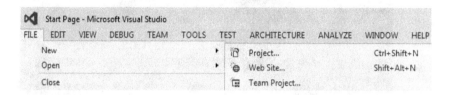

Fig 1.3

- From the options that appear, choose "Console Application." In the "Name" and "Location" text fields at the bottom, enter the name and location of your choice. Keep the "Create directory for solution" option checked and click the "OK" button as shown in the following figure:

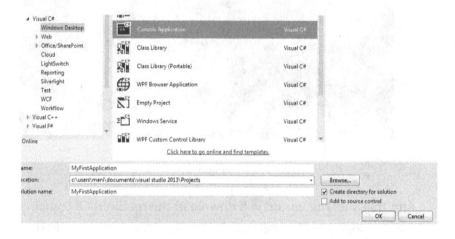

Fig 1.4

Note:

Your options might be different depending on the version of visual studio you have installed. However, remember that you have to select the "Console Application" type in any version you use.

- Once you click the "OK" button in figure 1.4, visual studio will automatically create a basic program for you. Replace the default code snippet with following:

```
using System;

namespaceMyFirstApplication
{
class Program
    {
static void Main(string[] args)
        {

Console.WriteLine("Welcome to C#");
Console.Read();


        }
    }
}
```

- Click on the "Start" button next to the green triangle in the tool bar. This is highlighted with a yellow rectangle in Fig 1.5. You will see the output of your code on the console. The string "Welcome to C#" which you wrote inside the "Console.WriteLine" method will be displayed on screen.

```
BUILD   DEBUG   TEAM   TOOLS   TEST   ARCHITECTURE   ANALYZE   WINDOW   HELP
   - Start - - Debug - Any CPU

Program.cs*  Start
 MyFirstApplication                    MyFirstApplication.Program                    Main(string[] args)
    using System;

 namespace MyFirstApplication
 {
     class Program
     {
         static void Main(string[] args)
         {

             Console.WriteLine("Welcome to C#");
             Console.Read();

         }
     }
 }
```

Fig 1.5

In the code in Fig 1.5, just keep in mind that everything in C# happens inside a class. The "Program" class is where code execution starts, since it contains the "Main" method. When you run a program, the "static void Main (string [] args)" method is called. The first statement which executes is the first statement inside the "Main" method. To add a new class to an existing project, simply right click the project name =>Add => Class.

You've completed the first chapter. In this chapter, you learned how to download an IDE, which is used for developing C# applications. You also developed your first C# application, which prints a string on the console screen. In the next chapter, we shall see what type of data a C# program can store and what operations can be performed on that data.

8

Chapter 2: Data Types and Operators

Every program needs to store some data and perform some functionality on the data. In C#, data is stored in data types, and operations are performed on the data using C# operators. In this chapter, we will take a look at some of the most commonly used data types, as well as the operators which operate on the data to help us achieve some meaningful functionality.

Contents

- **Data types in C#**
- **Operators in C#**

1- Data Types in C#

The following table demonstrates the usage of each data type along with the range of data that each data type can store.

Type	Represents	Range
bool	Boolean value	True or False
byte	8-bit unsigned integer	0 to 255
char	16-bit Unicode character	U +0000 to U +ffff
decimal	128-bit precise decimal values with 28-29 significant digits	(-7.9 x 1028 to 7.9 x 1028) / 100 to 28
double	64-bit double-precision floating point type	(+/-)5.0 x 10-324 to (+/-)1.7 x 10308
float	32-bit single-precision floating point type	-3.4 x 1038 to + 3.4 x 1038
int	32-bit signed integer type	-2,147,483,648 to 2,147,483,647
long	64-bit signed integer type	-923,372,036,854,775,808 to 9,223,372,036,854,775,807

sbyte	8-bit signed integer type	-128 to 127
short	16-bit signed integer type	-32,768 to 32,767
uint	32-bit unsigned integer type	0 to 4,294,967,295
ulong	64-bit unsigned integer type	0 to 18,446,744,073,709,551,615
ushort	16-bit unsigned integer type	0 to 65,535

Table 1.0

2- Operators in C#

In this section we are going to take a bird's eye view of three types of operators in C#: Arithmetic Operators, Relational Operators, and Logical Operators.

- **Arithmetic Operators**

Arithmetic operators in C# perform the same functionality as they do in real life. These operators are used to perform various mathematical functions in C#. Arithmetic operators can only be applied to the operands of numeric and char data types. Table 1.1 enlists these operators along with their functionalities.

Operator	What they do
+	Addition and unary plus
-	Subtraction and unary minus
*	Multiplication
/	Division
%	Modulus
++	Increment a number
+=	Increment and assign
-=	Decrement and assign
*=	Multiply and assign
/=	Divide and Assign
%=	Modulus and Assign
--	Decrement a Number

- Table 1.1

Have a look at the first example of this chapter to see some of the arithmetic operators in action.

Example1:

```
using System;

namespaceMyFirstApplication
{
class Program
    {
static void Main(string[] args)
        {

int num1 = 10;
            int num2 = 5;

            int sum = num1 + num2;
            int sub = num1 - num2;
            intmulti = num1 * num2;
            int division = num1 / num2;
            int mod = num1 % num2;

Console.WriteLine(
"Addition:"+sum+"\nSubtraction:"+sub+

        "\nMultiplication:"+multi+"\nDivision"+

        division+"\nModulus:"+mod);


Console.Read();

        }
    }
}
```

Here in Example1, we have declared two integer type variables, num1 and num2. These two variables store integers 10 and 5, respectively. Next, we have declared five integer type variables that store the sum, minus, multiplication, division, and modulus of num1 and number2. Finally, these variables have been printed on the console screen using "Console.WriteLine". The output of the code in Example1 is as follows:

Output 1:

```
Addition:15
Subtraction:5
Multiplication:50
Division: 2
Modulus:0
```

- **Relational Operators**

In C#, relational operators are used for comparing and ordering two operands. Table 1.2 enlists C# relational operators along with their functionalities.

Operators	What they do
==	Compare for equality
!=	Compare for inequality
>	Compare if operator on the left is greater
<	Compare if operator on the left is smaller
>=	Compare if operator on the left is greater or equal to

14

<=	Compare if operator on the left is smaller or equal to

Table 1.2

Example 2 demonstrates the usage of relational operators in C#.

Example2:

```
using System;

namespaceMyFirstApplication
{
class Program
    {
static void Main(string[] args)
        {

int num1 = 10;
int num2 = 20;

if (num1 == num2)
            {
Console.WriteLine("Num1 is equal to Num2");
            }

if (num1 != num2)
            {
Console.WriteLine("Num1 is not equal to Num2");
            }
if (num1 > num2)
            {
Console.WriteLine("Num1 is greater than Num2");
            }
if (num1 < num2)
```

```
            {
Console.WriteLine("Num1 is smaller than Num2");
            }
if  (num1 >= num2)
            {
Console.WriteLine("Num1  is  greater  than  or  equal  to
Num2");
            }
if  (num1 <= num2)
            {
Console.WriteLine("Num1  is  smaller  than  or  equal  to
Num2");

            }
Console.Read();
        }
    }
}
```

In Example2, two integer type variables, num1 and num2, have been instantiated with some values; then, in order to compare them, all the relational operators have been sequentially applied to them. Do not worry if you are unable to understand the "if" statement followed by the opening and closing round brackets. We will discuss that in detail in the next chapter. The output of the code in Example2 is as follows:

Output2:

```
Num1 is not equal to Num2
Num1 is smaller than Num2
Num1 is smaller than or equal to Num2
```

1- Logical Operators

Logical operators operate only on Boolean operands. The result of logical operation is another Boolean value. Table 1.3 lists C# logical operators:

Operator	What they do?
&	Logical AND
|	Logical OR
^	XOR (Exclusive OR)
||	Short Circuit OR
&&	Short Circuit AND
!	Unary NOT
&=	AND Followed by Assignment
|=	OR Followed by Assignment
^=	XOR Followed by Assignment
==	Equal
!=	Not Equal
?:	Ternary operator used for If then else

Table 1.3

Exercise 2

Task:

Initialize three integers with random numbers. If the first integer is equal to the second integer and both the first and second integers are greater than the third integer, multiply the three. Otherwise, add the three. Display the result on console.

Solution

```
using System;

namespaceMyFirstApplication
{
class Program
    {
static void Main(string[] args)
        {
int num1 = 20;
                int num2 = 20;
                int num3 = 5;

                if( (num1 == num2) && (num1 >num3) &&
num2 > num3)
                    {
                        int result = num1* num2* num3;
                        Console.WriteLine(result);
                    }
                else
                    {
                        int result = num1 +num2 + num3;
                        Console.WriteLine(result);
                    }

Console.Read();
```

```
        }
    }
}
```

19

Chapter 3: Selection Statements

Logic building lies at the core of every program. Logic building involves making decisions. In our daily lives, we make decisions based on certain criteria. For instance, if the weather is rainy, we decide not to play outside; if the weather is foggy, we drive carefully. There are hundreds of small decisions which we have to make every day. In the same way, a computer program has to make decisions during execution. Based on those decisions, a particular piece of code is executed, leaving some other piece of code unexecuted. For instance, you might want your program to take input from the user about the weather and then recommend if the user should play outside or not. In C#, this is done via selection statements (also known as control statements). In this chapter we are going to study C# selection statements.

Contents

- **If/Else Statements**
- **Switch Statements**

1- If/Else Statements

The "if" statement is used to execute a piece of code if the "test-expression" entered in the body of the statement evaluates to be true. Example1 demonstrates the usage of "if" statements.

Example1:

```
using System;

namespaceMyCSharpApplication
{
class Program
    {
static void Main(string[] args)
        {

string weather = "sunny";
if (weather == "rainy")
            {
Console.WriteLine("Don't play outside, it's rainy.");
            }
if (weather == "sunny")
            {
Console.WriteLine("You    can    play    outside,    it's
sunny.");
            }

Console.Read();
        }
    }
}
```

In Example 1, we have initialized a string type variable "weather" to "sunny". We have then used two "if" statements. The first "if"

21

statement evaluates if the variable "weather" contains the value "rainy". This expression would return false because the variable "weather" contains the string "sunny". The control would shift to the next "if" statement, where the comparison of the variable "weather" will be made with the string "rainy". This expression will return true and the code block followed by this if statement will execute. The output of Example1 is shown as follows:

Output1:

```
You can play outside, it's sunny.
```

There is a problem with using "if" statements. If the expression in the first "if" statement returns true, the comparison with the proceeding "if" statements will still be made. This is not desirable in some cases. For instance what if we want that if "weather" is equal to "rainy", the next "if" statement which compares weather with "sunny", should not execute? In such scenarios we use "else" and "if/else" statements. Example2 demonstrates this concept.

Example2:

```
using System;

namespaceMyCSharpApplication
{
class Program
    {
static void Main(string[] args)
        {

string weather = "rainy";
if (weather == "rainy")
```

```
                {
Console.WriteLine("Don't play outside, it's rainy.");
                }
else if (weather == "sunny")
                {
Console.WriteLine("You    can    play    outside,    it's
sunny.");
                }
else
                {
Console.WriteLine("Weather cannot be determined, try
again.");
                }

Console.Read();
                }
        }
}
```

In Example2, the variable "weather" has been initialized to "rainy". Therefore, the first "if" statement would be executed. After the "if" statement, we have used an "if/else" statement to evaluate if "weather" is equal to "sunny". But since the first "if" statement is true, the condition in the "if/else" statement would not execute, unlike multiple "if" statements where the conditions in proceeding statements are also evaluated, even if the first "if" statement is true. You can use as many "if/else" blocks after the "if" statement. You can also use one "else" statement after the "if" statement if you have to make a selection between two code blocks based on one condition. The output of Example2 is as follows:

Output2:

```
Don't play outside, it's rainy.
```

2- Switch Statement

"If/else" statements are good to use if you have to make a small number of comparisons. However, in the case of a larger number of comparisons, switch statements are a better alternative. To see a "switch statement" at work, let's jump straight to the third example of this chapter.

Example3:

```
using System;

namespaceMyCSharpApplication
{
class Program
    {
static void Main(string[] args)
        {

string weather = "cloudy";

switch (weather)
        {
case "rainy":
Console.WriteLine("Don't play outside, it's rainy.");
break;
case "sunny":
Console.WriteLine("You    can    play    outside.    It's
sunny.");
break;
case "cloudy":
```

```
Debug.WriteLine("Play  but  take  your  umbrella  with
you, it's cloudy.");
break;

default:
Console.WriteLine("Weather cannot be determined");
break;
            }

Console.Read();
        }
    }
}
```

Switch statements start with a keyword "switch" followed by a pair of opening and closing round brackets. Inside these brackets, we enter the variable which we want to compare. In Example3, we initialized the variable "weather" and assigned it the string "cloudy". Inside the switch statement there are multiple case statements. Each case has a string value mentioned with it followed by a colon. Underneath every case statement, a code segment has been added. The code segment of that case will be executed based on whose value matches with the string variable "weather" mentioned in the opening and closing round brackets of the switch statement. Since the "weather" variable contains the string "cloudy", the code segment of third case statement would be executed. It is also noteworthy that after every case statement, the "break" keyword has been mentioned. This is to avoid further case comparisons, in case a "case" statement has already been matched. If none of the case matches with the variable of the switch statement, the code after the "default" statement is executed which is mentioned in the end. The output of the code in Example3 is as follows:

Output3:

```
Play but take your umbrella with you, it's cloudy.
```

Exercise 3

Task:

Initialize an integer type variable to a random value. Write a switch statement containing four cases. One of the case values should match the integer variable you initialized. In each case statement code segment, display different gifts. Display PS4 as a gift against the integer value you initialized.

Solution

```
using System;
usingSystem.Diagnostics;

namespaceMyCSharpApplication
{
class Program
    {
static void Main(string[] args)
        {

int lottery = 451876;

switch (lottery)
            {
case 467681:
Console.WriteLine("You won a mobile set.");
break;
```

```
case 451876:
Console.WriteLine("You won a PS4.");
break;
case 742167:
Debug.WriteLine("Sorry you won nothing.");
break;

case 741963:
Debug.WriteLine("You won a cinema ticket");
break;
default:
Console.WriteLine("Sorry you won nothing.");
break;
            }

Console.Read();
        }
    }
}
```

Chapter 4: Iteration Statements

While writing a program, you might want to repeatedly execute a particular piece of code. One way is to write that piece of code the number of times you want to repeatedly execute it. However, this approach is extremely unprofessional, resulting in unnecessarily verbose code. To address this problem, iteration statements were introduced. The concept of iteration statements dates back to the earliest programming languages. Their syntax may differ in different languages, but the core concept remains the same; they are meant to execute the code a number of times as specified by developer. Iteration statements are often referred as "loops" since they execute code repeatedly in the form of loops.

C# contains four types of iteration statements. In this chapter, we are going to study each of those types.

Content

- **"For" loop**
- **"While" Loop**
- **"Do While" Loop**

- **"Foreach" Loop**

1- The "For" Loop

"For" loops allow developers to write a piece of code which executes exactly the number of times as specified by the developer. This loop is perfect to use when you know the exact number of iterations you want your code to go through. For instance, if you want to print your name ten times on the screen, a "for loop" is the solution since you already know that there will be ten iterations of the code which prints your name on the screen. To see a "for loop" in action, have a look at the first example of this chapter.

Example1:

```
using System;

namespaceMyCSharpApplication
{
class Program
    {
static void Main(string[] args)
        {
for (inti = 1; i<= 10; i++)
            {
Console.WriteLine("Welcome to C#");
            }
Console.Read();
        }
    }
}
```

Pay attention to the syntax of the "for loop"; it starts with an opening round bracket. Inside the round bracket we have three expressions separated by semicolons. The first expression, "i=1", is the initialization-clause which means that loop starts with "i=1". This is evaluated only once. The second expression "i<=10" is the condition-clause, which says that the loop will keep executing until this condition returns true. After evaluating the condition-clause, the body of the loop (which is inside the curly brackets followed by the closing round bracket) executes. The last expression inside the round bracket is "i++". This is called the iteration clause; each time the body of the loop executes, this clause executes and the control again shifts to the "condition-clause". The loop keeps executing until the condition-clause returns true. In Example1, the loop starts from "i=1" and keeps executing until "i" is less than or equal to ten, with increments of 1 in each execution. This means that the loop would execute 10 times. Each time, the statement "Welcome to C#" will be printed on the console, so the output would contain "Welcome to C#" printed on screen 10 times.

Output 1:

```
Welcome to C#
Welcome to C#
Welcome to C#
Welcome to C#
Welcome to C#
Welcome to C#
Welcome to C#
Welcome to C#
Welcome to C#
Welcome to C#
```

2- "While" Loop

A "while" loop keeps executing until a certain condition becomes true. "While" loop should be used when you do not exactly know that how many times you want to execute a particular piece of code. Rather, you want your loop to execute until a specific condition becomes true or false. In Example2, we will again print "Welcome to C#" on screen ten times, but this time using "while loop".

Example2:

```
using System;

namespaceMyCSharpApplication
{
class Program
    {
static void Main(string[] args)
        {
inti = 1;
while (i<=10)
            {
Console.WriteLine("Welcome to C#");
i++;

            }
Console.Read();
        }
    }
}
```

In Example2, we can see that the "while" loop only has a condition-clause inside the round brackets. This is because the "while" loop doesn't know how many times it has to execute. All it knows is that, unless the condition-clause becomes true, it has to execute. If you write "true" in the condition-clause, the "while" loop will keep executing forever.

Output2:

```
Welcome to C#
Welcome to C#
Welcome to C#
Welcome to C#
Welcome to C#
Welcome to C#
Welcome to C#
Welcome to C#
Welcome to C#
Welcome to C#
```

3- "Do While" Loop

The "do while" loop is similar to the "while" loop in functionality. It depends only upon the condition clause. However, unlike the "while" loop, the "do while" loop executes at least once. This is because the condition clause of the "do while" loop is evaluated at the end of the code block. This way, the code block executes at least once before the condition-clause is evaluated. Example3 demonstrates this process.

Example3:

```
using System;

namespaceMyCSharpApplication
{
class Program
    {
static void Main(string[] args)
```

```
        {
inti = 1;

do
            {
Console.WriteLine("Welcome to C#");
i++;

            }
while (i<= 10) ;

Console.Read();
        }
    }
}
```

In Example3, you can see that the body of the loop starts with a keyword, "do", followed by the code block. At the end of the code block you can see the "while" keyword. The condition clause is evaluated here, but before reaching this point of code, the loop has executed at least once. The output will again display "Welcome to C#" on the console, but this time using the "do while" loop.

Output3:

```
Welcome to C#
Welcome to C#
Welcome to C#
Welcome to C#
Welcome to C#
Welcome to C#
Welcome to C#
Welcome to C#
Welcome to C#
```

4- "Foreach" Loop

In C#, the "foreach" loop iterates over all those objects which can be enumerated. Most of the .NET types which contain list or sets of elements are enumerable. For example, arrays and strings. They can be iterated using a "foreach" loop since they store collections of items. This concept has been demonstrated in Example4.

Example4:

```
using System;

namespaceMyCSharpApplication
{
class Program
    {
static void Main(string[] args)
        {

foreach (char c in "Welcome to C#")
            {
Console.WriteLine(c);


            }

Console.Read();
        }
    }
}
```

Pay attention to the body of the "foreach" loop. It starts with a variable, which is "char c" in this case. Here, the type used for the variable is char because we are iterating over the string "Welcome to

34

C#" and each item of this string is of the "char" type. Then we used the keyword "in". This keyword has to be used whenever you are using a "foreach" loop to iterate over a collection. Finally, we have to enter the name of the collection on which we want to enumerate. The "foreach" loop executes a number of times equal to the items inside the collection. In the code block, we printed each character of the string "Welcome to C#" on a new line.

Output4:

```
W
e
l
c
o
m
e

t
o

C
#
```

Exercise 4

Task:

Using a "while" loop, display the sum of all the even numbers between 0 and 100 (inclusive).

Solution:

```
using System;
usingSystem.Diagnostics;

namespaceMyCSharpApplication
{
class Program
    {
static void Main(string[] args)
        {

inti = 0;
int sum = 0;
while (i<= 100)
            {
if (i % 2 == 0)
              {
sum = sum + i;
              }
i++;
            }
Console.WriteLine("Sum of even numbers between 0 and
100 is:"+sum);
Console.Read();
        }
    }
}
```

Chapter 5: Arrays

Suppose you have to store the salaries of three employees. You can declare three integer type variables which can store those salaries. What if you have to store the salaries of one hundred employees? Will you declare one hundred integer type variables and then individually store the salary of each employee in one variable? This is one solution. However, accessing variables this way is very cumbersome. Also, this approach results in verbose code. A better approach is to use C# arrays. An array contains a collection of items of a particular type. Arrays store data in contiguous memory locations which improves its efficiency. Each item in an array is called.

Contents:

- **Array Syntax**
- **One-dimensional Array**
- **Two-dimensional Array**

1- Array Syntax

An array has the following syntax:

```
type [] array-name = new type [size];
```

An array starts with the type of element it is going to store, followed by a square bracket and finally the name of the array. At this point in time, an array is only declared and no memory locations are reserved for it. To initialize an array, you use the "new" keyword followed by the type of the array. This is followed by square brackets, and, inside those square brackets, you specify the size of the array. The size specifies the number of elements an array can store. The following piece of code specifies how to initialize an integer type array named salaries with a size of 10.

```
int [] salaries = new int [10];
```

2- One-Dimensional Array

An array which stores elements in one direction, i.e. in the form of a column or row, is called a one-dimensional array. The "salaries" array which we declared in the last section was a one-dimensional array. A one-dimensional array is initialized using one square bracket after the array type. To see a one-dimensional array in action, have a look at the first example of this chapter.

Example1:

```
using System;

namespaceMyCSharpApplication
{
class Program
    {
```

```
static void Main(string[] args)
    {

int[] salaries = new int[10] { 78, 15, 27, 87, 56,
74, 12, 36, 98, 41 };


int a = salaries[0];
int b = salaries[5];

Console.WriteLine(a + b);

salaries[0] = 25;
salaries[5] = 25;


        a = salaries[0];
        b = salaries[5];

Console.WriteLine(a + b);

Console.Read();
    }
  }
}
```

In Example1, we initialized the array "salaries" and stored 10 elements in this array at initialization time. This is one way to store elements in the array. You initialize the array and, on the same line, you enter the elements inside the curly brackets that follow after the square brackets containing the size. Inside the curly bracket, you separate each element with a comma. An array has a zero based storage index. This means that the first element of the array is stored at 0th index while the last element is stored at n-1st index, where n is the size of the array. To access the element at any index, you use the name of the array followed by square brackets. Inside the square brackets, you mention the index. For instance, in Example1, the element at the 0th index of the salaries array is stored in integer variable "a", while the element at the 5th index is stored in variable "b". On the console, the sum of these two variables is printed. Then the array indexes zero and five are updated with value 25. On the console window, their sum is again printed, which now contains the updated value. The output of the code in Example1 is shown below.

Output1:

```
152
50
```

In Chapter 4, we studied the "foreach" loop, which can be used to iterate over any set or list of items. In addition to the "foreach" loop, the "for" loop can also be used to iterate over an array. In Example2, we shall see how an array can be iterated via "for" and "foreach" loops.

Example2:

```
using System;

namespaceMyCSharpApplication
{
class Program
    {
static void Main(string[] args)
        {

int[] salaries = new int[10] { 78, 15, 27, 87, 56,
74, 12, 36, 98, 41 };
```

```
for (inti = 0; i< 10; i++ )
            {
Console.Write(salaries[i] + " ");
            }

Console.WriteLine();

foreach (int n in salaries)
            {
Console.Write(n+" ");
            }

Console.Read();
          }
        }
}
```

In Example2, the "salaries" array has again been initialized with some random variables. We first iterated the array with a "for" loop, then we iterated over the "salaries" array using a "foreach" loop. The output of the code in Example2 is as follows.

Output2:

```
78  15  27  87  56  74  12  36  98  41
78  15  27  87  56  74  12  36  98  41
```

3- Two-dimensional Array

A one-dimensional array stores data in the form of a single column or row. A two-dimensional array, often referred as an array of arrays, stores data in the form of multiple rows and columns. Data is stored in the memory in the form of a matrix. To initialize a two-dimensional array, you simply have to put a comma inside the square bracket that follows after the type of the array. On the left side, after the new keyword and inside the square brackets, you have to mention the number of rows and columns that the array will contain. Rows and columns should be separated by commas. Look at Example3 to see two-dimensional arrays in action.

Example3:

```
using System;

namespaceMyCSharpApplication
{
class Program
    {
static void Main(string[] args)
        {

int[,] salaries = new int [2,3];

salaries[0,0] = 10; // First row first column
salaries[0,1] = 20; // First row second column
salaries[0, 2] = 30; // First row third column

salaries[1, 0] = 40; // 2nd row first column
salaries[1, 1] = 50; // 2nd row second column
salaries[1, 2] = 60; // 2nd row third column

for (inti = 0; i< 2; i++)
            {
for (int j = 0; j < 3; j++)
                {
```

```
Console.Write(salaries[i, j]+"  ");
                    }
Console.WriteLine();
              }
Console.Read();
          }
      }
}
```

In Example1, we initialized a two-dimensional array, "salaries", with two rows and three columns. We then accessed each index and stored some random integer values. To access a particular index of a two-dimensional array, you write the name of the array followed by the square bracket. Inside the square brackets, you first enter the row number, then comma, and then the column number. To iterate over a two-dimensional array requires nested "for" loops where the outer loop iterates over each row and the inner loop iterates over each column. This is demonstrated in Example3. The output of the code in Example3 is as follows.

Output3:

```
10   20   30
40   50   60
```

Exercise 5

Task:

Using nested "for" loops, store the table of 2,3,4, and 5 in a two-dimensional array and then display the elements of the array on screen.

Solution

```
using System;

namespaceMyCSharpApplication
{
class Program
    {
static void Main(string[] args)
        {

int[,] tables = new int [4,10];

for (inti = 2; i< 6; i++)
            {
for (int j = 0; j <10; j++)
                {
tables[i-2,j] = i*(j+1);


                }
            }

for (inti = 0; i< 4; i++)
            {
for (int j = 0; j < 10; j++)
                {
Console.Write(tables[i, j]+"   ");
                }
```

```
Console.WriteLine();
            }
Console.Read();
        }
    }
}
```

Chapter 6: Objects and Classes

In the first five chapters, we covered most of the basic C# programming concepts. From this chapter onwards, we are going to study some of the advanced programming concepts, starting with object oriented programming. In object oriented programming (OOP), all the software components are viewed in the context of real world objects. For instance, you are developing some car racing game; you will identify the objects in the real world car racing. A driver can be an object, a car can be another object, and steering is also an object. When you develop your game you will create these objects in your program. These objects will interact with each other, resulting in fully functional racing car game. This is just a crude example of how modules are developed in OOP programming. OOP offers advantages such as code modularity, usability, and maintainability.

Contents

- **Objects and Classes**
- **Constructor**

1- Objects and Classes

Anything which has some properties and can perform some functions is worthy of being implemented as an object in an OOP. As aforementioned, a player in a racing car game can be considered an object since it contains properties like a name, age, country, etc. A player can also perform functions like starting the car, increasing the speed, turning left, turning right, etc. A player is a perfect candidate for being implemented as an object.

Before diving into the code, an important distinction needs to be made here between a class and an object. A class is similar to a blue print. It has no physical existence in the memory. Class depicts how the object looks. Multiple objects can be created from one class. An object, on the other hand, has an actual physical existence in the memory. A class is like a blueprint while an object is the house built according to that blueprint.

To see how objects are created, have a look at the first example of this chapter.

Example1:

Add a new class to your project and name it "Player". The contents of the player class should be exactly like the following code snippet.

```
class Player
    {
string name;
int age;
string country;
    }
```

This is the structure of the player class. From this structure, it can be assumed that the object of the class will contain three variables: name, age, and country. The memory occupied by the object of the player will be roughly equal to the sum of the memories occupied by the variables name, age, and country. The "Player" class would have been created in the same namespace in which your "Program" class resides.

Open the "Program" class code and make following changes.

```
using System;

namespaceMyCSharpApplication
{
class Program
    {
static void Main(string[] args)
        {
            Player p = new Player();
            p.name = "Alan";
p.age = 25;
p.country = "USA";

Console.WriteLine(p.name +","+p.age+","+p.country);

Console.Read();
        }
    }
}
```

In the Program.cs file above, we created an object "p" in the "Player" class. To create an object of any class, use the "new" keyword followed by the constructor of the class. We will dig deeper into constructors in the next section. For now, assume that "Player()" is the default constructor of the "Player" class. Calling "new" followed

48

by the constructor of any class creates an object of that class in memory and returns its reference. This reference can be stored in the variable of that class. In Example1, we created a variable "p" in class "Player". This variable "p" stores the reference of the object in the "Player" class. To access the members of an object, use the reference variable then a dot (.) followed by the property that you want to access. For instance, if you want to access the name of the object "p", you will use p.name. In this way, we stored three random values in name, age, and country. Finally, we print these values on the output console.

Output1:

```
Alan,25,USA
```

2- Constructor

A constructor is a function which creates an object of a class and returns its reference to the calling function. The name of the constructor is exactly the same as the name of the class in which it is written. A constructor has no return type, not even void. A constructor can also be used to initialize the member variables of the class when the object is being created. In the second example of this chapter, we will see how a constructor can be used to initialize member variables.

Example2:

Make the following changes in the "Player" class you created in Example1.

```
using System;
```

```
namespaceMyCSharpApplication
{
class Player
    {
public string name;
publicint age;
public string country;

public Player()
        {
name = "Scott";
age = 30;
country = "UK";


        }
    }
}
```

In the above code, we created a constructor which initializes the variables name, age, and country. Name becomes "Scott", age becomes "30", and country becomes "UK". When the object of this class is created calling this constructor, these three variables will automatically be initialized and will be readily available for printing on screen. To see their values on the console, make the following changes in the "Program" class.

```
using System;

namespaceMyCSharpApplication
{
class Program
    {
static void Main(string[] args)
```

```
        {
            Player p = new Player();


Console.WriteLine(p.name +", "+p.age+", "+p.country);
Console.Read();
        }
    }
}
```

The output of the code in Example2 is as follows:

Output2:

```
Scott,30,UK
```

- **Parameterized Constructor**

You can also initialize the member variables of the class using a constructor by passing arguments to the constructor while creating the object of the class. The constructor, which takes parameter from the calling function, is called a parameterized constructor. Example3 demonstrates usage of the parameterized constructor in C#.

Example3:

Make the following changes in the Player class:

```
using System;

namespaceMyCSharpApplication
{
class Player
    {
```

```
public string name;
publicint age;
public string country;

public Player(string name, int age, string country)
        {
              this.name = name;
this.age = age;
this.country = country;


        }
    }
}
```

In the above code snippet, we have entered three variables in the round brackets after the constructor name. These are the parameters, which are separated by commas. To call this constructor, we have to pass three parameters in the call to constructor. These parameters should match the parameter type in the constructor declaration. Also, the order of the passed parameters should match the order of the parameters in the constructor declaration. For instance, in the call to this parameterized constructor, the first parameter should be string, the second should be integer, and the third should be again string. Make the following changes in the "Program" class to see how this works.

```
using System;

namespaceMyCSharpApplication
{
class Program
    {
static void Main(string[] args)
```

```
        {
            Player p = new Player("Joseph", 35,
"Italy");


Console.WriteLine(p.name +","+p.age+","+p.country);
Console.Read();
        }
    }
}
```

The output of the code in Example3 is as follows:

Output3:

```
Joseph,35,Italy
```

- **Overloaded Constructor**

You can have two or more parameterized constructors in your class. When the object of the class is created, the constructor whose parameters match with the parameter in the call to the constructor would be called. This concept sounds confusing at first. The fourth example of this chapter demonstrates the concept of an overloaded constructor.

Example4:

Make the following changes in the "Player" class.

Player.cs

```
using System;


namespaceMyCSharpApplication
{
class Player
    {
public string name;
publicint age;
public string country;

public Player(string name, int age, string country)
        {
            this.name = name;
this.age = age;
this.country = country;


        }

public Player(string name)
        {
            this.name = name;
        }
    }
}
```

In the "Player" class, you can see that now there are two parameterized constructors. The first constructor is similar to the one in Example3 and it takes three parameters. The second constructor takes one parameter. The constructor that is called when an object is created depends on the call to the constructor. If the call contains one string type parameter, the second constructor will be called. However, if the call contains three parameters(string, int, string), the first constructor would be called.

Make the following changes in the "Program" class to see difference between the calls to the two constructors in the "Player" class.

Program.cs

```
using System;

namespaceMyCSharpApplication
{
class Program
    {
static void Main(string[] args)
        {
            Player  p  =  new  Player("Joseph",  35,
"Italy");

            Player p2 = new Player("Susan");
            p2.age = 40;
            p2.country = "France";

        Console.WriteLine(p.name + "," + p.age + "," +
p.country);
Console.WriteLine(p2.name
+","+p2.age+","+p2.country);


Console.Read();
        }
    }
}
```

The output of the code in Example4 is as follows:

```
Joseph,35,Italy
Susan,40,France
```

Exercise 6

Task:

Create a class named "Product" with three properties: name, price, and category. Add a parameterized constructor which initializes these three properties. Add another constructor which initializes the first two properties. In the "Program" class, create two objects of "Product" class by calling the two overloaded constructors of the "Player" class. Display the properties of both objects on the console.

Solution:

Product Class:

```
using System;
usingSystem.Collections.Generic;
usingSystem.Linq;
usingSystem.Text;
usingSystem.Threading.Tasks;

namespaceMyCSharpApplication
{
class Product
    {
public string name;
```

```
publicint price;
public string category;

public    Product(string    name,    int    price,    string
category)
        {
              this.name = name;
this.price = price;
this.category = category;
        }

public Product(string name, int price)
        {
              this.name = name;
this.price = price;
        }


    }
}
```

Program Class

```
using System;

namespaceMyCSharpApplication
{
class Program
    {
static void Main(string[] args)
        {
            Product  p  =  new  Product("Laptop",  40,
"Electronics");

            Product p2 = new Product("Apple", 2);
            p2.category = "Fruits";


Console.WriteLine(p2.name
+","+p2.price+","+p2.category);

Console.WriteLine(p.name  +  ","  +  p.price  +  ","  +
p.category);

Console.Read();
        }
    }
}
```

Chapter 7: Access Modifiers and Methods

In the last chapter, we studied what objects and classes are and how the member variables of a class can be initialized via constructor. We also studied different types of constructors. In this chapter, we are going to study how objects act to perform certain functionalities. In object oriented programming (OOP), this is achieved via methods. However, before diving into the details of methods, we shall study another important concept: access modifiers in C#.

Contents

- **Access Modifiers**
- **Methods in C#**

1- Access Modifiers

From the beginning of this book, we have been using the keyword "public" with variables. This is one of the five access modifiers available in C#. Access modifiers control access to a particular variable. For instance, a member variable marked "public" can be accessed anywhere. However, a variable marked "private" is accessible only within the class in which it exists. Table 1.0 contains C#'s five access modifiers along with their functionalities.

Access Modifier	Functionality
public	Accessible everywhere
internal	Accessible only to the classes within the assembly and friend assemblies
protected	Accessible only within the class and its derived classes
private	Accessible only within the class
Protected-internal	Accessible where protected or internal are accessible

2- Methods

As aforementioned, C# classes and objects act via methods. To understand the concept of methods in C#, let's jump straight to the first example of this chapter.

Example1:

Add a new class named "Product" to the existing project. The contents of the "Product" class should be similar to the following code snippet.

Product.cs

```
using System;


namespaceMyCSharpApplication
{
class Product
    {
        public string name;
public   int price;
public string category;

public   Product(string   name,   int   price,   string
category)
        {
            this.name = name;
this.price = price;
this.category = category;
        }

public void IncreasePrice()
        {
price += 10;
        }


    }
}
```

The produce class contains three member variables: name, price, and category. The class contains a constructor which initializes these three variables. After the constructor, we have added a method named "IncreasePrice". The syntax of a method is simple; it starts with an access modifier, which is public in this case. After that, the return type of the method is mentioned. A return type is the type of the value returned by the method. Since our "IncreasePrice" method doesn't return any value, we specified its return type as void. After the return type, the name of the method is written (in our case, this is "IncreasePrice"). The opening and closing round brackets contain parameters. Since we don't want our "IncreasePrice" method to accept any parameter, we left the brackets empty. Notice that the method declaration is quite similar to the constructor declaration. A constructor is, in fact, a method with no return type. A method is called using the object of the class by the appending dot operator followed by the method name after the object of the class. Modify the "Program" class so that it looks like the one in following code snippet.

<u>Program.cs</u>

```
using System;

namespaceMyCSharpApplication
{
class Program
    {
static void Main(string[] args)
        {
            Product  p  =  new  Product("Grapes",  40,
"Food");

Console.WriteLine("The  price  of  product  "+p.name+  "
is: "+p.price);


p.IncreasePrice();
```

```
Console.WriteLine("The   new   price   of   product   "   +
p.name + " is: " + p.price);

Console.Read();
        }
    }
}
```

In the "Program", we created the object of "Product" class using a
parameterized constructor. The initial value of the variable "price" is
set to 40. We displayed this price on the console. Then we called the
"IncreasePrice" method on the object "p" of the "Product" class. The
value of the "price" variable is incremented by 10 every time the
"IncreasePrice" method is called. Since we called this method only
once, the price is incremented by 10 only once; the new price would
be 40+10 = 50. We then printed this new price on the console just to
make sure the price was incremented. The output of the code in
Example1 is as follows:

Output1:

```
The price of product Grapes is: 40
The new price of product Grapes is: 50
```

- **Passing Parameters to a Method**

Just like we have parameterized constructors, we also have
parameterized methods. For instance, instead of increasing the price
of the price variable by 10 every time, we can also pass a value of our
choice. Types of parameters which a method can accept are
mentioned in the round brackets that follow the method name. In

the second example, we will see how we can increase the price by the value of our choice by passing the value as a parameter to the "IncreasePrice" method.

Example2:

Change the code in the "Product" and "Program" classes as follows:

Product.cs

```
using System;

namespaceMyCSharpApplication
{
class Product
    {
public string name;
public  int price;
public string category;

public   Product(string   name,   int   price,   string
category)
        {
            this.name = name;
this.price = price;
this.category = category;
        }

public void IncreasePrice(int price)
        {
this.price += price;
        }
    }
}
```

Program.cs

```
using System;

namespaceMyCSharpApplication
{
class Program
    {
static void Main(string[] args)
        {
            Product  p  =  new  Product("Grapes",  40,
"Food");

Console.WriteLine("The  price  of  product  "+p.name+  "
is: "+p.price);

p.IncreasePrice(25);

Console.WriteLine("The  new  price  of  product  "  +
p.name + " is: " + p.price);

Console.Read();
        }
    }
}
```

Output2:

```
The price of product Grapes is: 40
The new price of product Grapes is: 65
```

- **Returning Values From Method**

In both of our first two examples, the method "IncreasePrice" did not return any value. The return type of the method was void. However, we can also force a method to return a value by changing its return type. For instance, we can retrieve the increased price from the "IncreasePrice" method by changing its return type to "int" and then using "return" at the end of the method, followed by the value to be returned. This is explained in the following example.

Example3:

Change the code in the "Product" and "Program" classes as follows:

Product.cs

```
using System;

namespaceMyCSharpApplication
{
class Product
    {
public string name;
public  int price;
public string category;

public   Product(string   name,   int   price,   string
category)
        {
            this.name = name;
this.price = price;
this.category = category;
        }

publicintIncreasePrice(int price)
        {
```

```
this.price += price;

returnthis.price;
        }
    }
}
```

Program.cs

```
using System;

namespaceMyCSharpApplication
{
class Program
    {
static void Main(string[] args)
        {
            Product  p  =  new  Product("Grapes",  40,
"Food");

Console.WriteLine("The   price   of   product   "+p.name+
"is: "+p.price);

Console.WriteLine("The   new   price   of   product   "   +
p.name + "is: " + p.IncreasePrice(20));

Console.Read();
        }
    }
}
```

Output3:

```
The price of product Grapesis: 40
The new price of product Grapesis: 60
```

Exercise 7

Task:

Create a class named "Car". Create two variables named "name" and "speed" inside the class. Initialize these variables using a parameterized constructor. Create a method inside the "Car" class. This method should accept an integer value and decrease the speed of the car by that value. The method should return the decreased speed to the calling function. In the "Program" class, display the decreased speed on console.

Solution:

Car Class:

```csharp
using System;
usingSystem.Collections.Generic;


namespaceMyCSharpApplication
{
class Car
    {
public string name;
publicint speed;

public Car(string name, int speed)
        {
                this.name = name;
this.speed = speed;
        }

publicintDecreaseSpeed(int speed)
        {
this.speed -= speed;
returnthis.speed;
        }
    }
}
```

Program Class:

```
using System;
usingSystem.Diagnostics;


namespaceMyCSharpApplication
{
class Program
    {
static void Main(string[] args)
        {
            Car c = new Car("Ford", 105);

Console.WriteLine("Initial    Speed    of    car    is
"+c.speed);

Console.WriteLine("Decreased  Speed  of  car  is   " +
c.DecreaseSpeed(15));

Console.Read();
        }
    }
}
```

Chapter 8: Inheritance & Polymorphism

In the last two chapters, we covered basic object oriented concepts (OOP). In this chapter, we are going to study two advanced OOPs: Inheritance and Polymorphism. Like all the other OOP concepts, inheritance in OOP is similar to the concept of real world inheritance. A child inherits some of the traits of his/her parents while also having some traits specific to him/her. In object oriented programming, the concept is similar. Inheritance also exists between different classes and is marked by an Is-A relationship. For instance, a "laptop" is a product, a "car" is a vehicle, and an "employee" is a person. Here, "laptop" is a child class of product, "car" is child of vehicle, and "employee" is a child class of person. The concept of polymorphism is based on inheritance; we will study that in a later section.

Contents

- **Inheritance**
- **Polymorphism**

1- Inheritance

The idea of inheritance is that all the traits that are common between the child classes are implemented in the parent class, while traits that are specific to individual child classes are implemented in the respective child classes. For instance, take a parent product class and its child software and hardware product. Both software and hardware products have a name and price. Therefore, we can include both name and price properties in the parent product class. Classes that inherit the parent class have all the attributes of the parent class by default. However, software has no weight while hardware product has some weight. This means that the attribute weight is unique to hardware class; therefore, it cannot be implemented in the parent class. Similarly, we assume that software has a version number while hardware has no version number. Here, version is unique to the software class and cannot be implemented in the parent class. This scenario has been implemented in Example1.

Example1:

Add three classes(Product, Hardware, and Software) to your project. The code markup of these three classes should be as follows:

Product.cs

```
using System;


namespaceMyCSharpApplication
{
class Product
    {
public string name;
public  int price;
```

```
        }
}
```

In the Product class, we added only two attributes: name and price.

Software.cs

```
using System;

namespaceMyCSharpApplication
{
class Software : Product
    {
publicint version;

public Software(string name, int price, int version)
        {
                this.name = name;
this.price = price;
this.version = version;
        }
    }
}
```

Have a look at the declaration of the software class. After the name of the class, we appended a semicolon followed by "Product". This is how the child class inherits the parent class. You have to append a semicolon after the child class name followed by the class name which you want your child class to inherit. In the above code, the "Software" class is inheriting the "Product" class. In the software classes, we added only one attribute named "version". Then we added a parameterized constructor with three parameters. Inside the constructor, we initialized name, price, and version attributes. Notice that the "Software" class doesn't contain name and price attributes, but since it is inheriting the "Product" class, which contains these attributes, the child "Software" class has these attributes by default. In the same way, we inherited the "Hardware" class from the "Product" class and initialized its attributes.

Hardware.cs

```
using System;

namespaceMyCSharpApplication
{
class Hardware : Product
    {
publicint weight;

public Hardware(string name, int price, int weight)
        {
            this.name = name;
this.price = price;
this.weight = weight;

        }

    }
}
```

In the "Program" class, we create objects of both the "Software" and "Hardware" classes using their parameterized constructors and then display the names of both of the objects.

Program.cs

```
using System;

namespaceMyCSharpApplication
{
class Program
    {
static void Main(string[] args)
        {

            Software   s  =  new  Software("windows  7",
150, 3);
            Hardware  h = new  Hardware("Laptop",  500,
2);

Console.WriteLine("You bought: " + s.name + " and " +
h.name);

Console.Read();
        }
    }
}
```

Output1:

```
You bought: windows 7 and Laptop
```

2- Polymorphism

The object of the parent class can hold objects of child classes. The parent class acts differently depending on the reference of the object it is storing. This concept lies in the basis of polymorphism. Suppose the "Product" class has a method, "DisplayProduct", which displays the name of the product on screen. Both the child classes

75

also have a method called "DisplayProduct". The method inside the "Software" class displaysname and version while the method inside the "Hardware" class displays name and price. Since the object of the "Product" class can store references of the "Product", "Software", and "Hardware" classes, the question arises here that if "DisplayProduct" method is called on the object, which method will be called? Will it be of "Product", "Software", or "Hardware" class? The answer is the "DisplayProduct" method will call the class whose reference is stored in the object of the "Product" class. This concept has been explained in Example2.

Example2

Make the following modification to the "Product", "Software", and "Hardware" classes added in Example1.

Product.cs

```
using System;

namespaceMyCSharpApplication
{
class Product
    {
public string name;
public  int price;

public virtual void DisplayProduct()
        {
Console.WriteLine("This is a parent class: " + name);
        }


    }
}
```

If child classes have to contain a method with the same name as in the parent class, that method has to be marked virtual in the parent class. This is why we marked the "DisplayProduct" method virtual in the parent class. When this method is added in the child class, it has to be marked with the keyword "override". This is shown in both the "Software" and "Hardware" classes.

Software.cs

```
using System;

namespaceMyCSharpApplication
{
class Software : Product
    {
publicint version;

public Software(string name, int price, int version)
        {
            this.name = name;
this.price = price;
this.version = version;
        }

public override void DisplayProduct()
        {
Console.WriteLine("You bought " + name + ", version
"+ version);
        }
    }
}
```

Hardware.cs

```
using System;

namespaceMyCSharpApplication
{
class Hardware : Product
    {
publicint weight;

public Hardware(string name, int price, int weight)
        {
            this.name = name;
this.price = price;
this.weight = weight;


        }

public override void DisplayProduct()
        {
Console.WriteLine("You bought " + name + ", weight "
+ weight);
        }


    }
}
```

In the "Program" class, we created the object of parent "Product" class and then stored references of the objects of the "Product", "Software", and "Hardware" classes in it. Then we called the "DisplayProduct" method sequentially. You will see that, in the output, different "DisplayProduct" methods will be called depending on the references stored in the "Product" class object.

Program.cs

```
using System;

namespaceMyCSharpApplication
{
class Program
    {
static void Main(string[] args)
        {

            Product p = new Product();
            p.name = "Apple";
p.price = 10;
p.DisplayProduct();

            p = new Software("windows 7", 150, 3);
p.DisplayProduct();

            p = new Hardware("Laptop", 500, 2);
p.DisplayProduct();

Console.Read();
        }
    }
}
```

Output2:

```
This is a parent class: Apple
You bought windows 7, version 3
You bought Laptop, weight 2
```

Exercise 8

Task:

Create a class named "Shape". Add one member variable, "name", to this class. Add a method called "DisplayName" which displays the variable name on console screen with the appropriate statement. Create two classes, "Triangle" and "Pentagon". Create parameterized constructors which initialize variable names in both the "Triangle" and "Pentagon" classes. These classes will implement their own "DisplayName" method. Using a test class, such as Program.cs, show how polymorphism can be achieved in this scenario.

Solution:

Shape Class:

```
using System;

namespaceMyCSharpApplication
{
class Shape
    {
public string name;

public virtual void DisplayName()
            {
                Console.WriteLine("This    is    a    parent
class named: " + name);
            }
    }
}
```

Triangle Class

```
using System;

namespaceMyCSharpApplication
{
class Triangle: Shape
    {

public Triangle (string name)
            {
                    this.name = name;
            }

        public override void DisplayName()
            {
                Console.WriteLine ("This  is  a  child
class named: " + name);
            }


    }
}
```

Pentagon Class

```
using System;


namespaceMyCSharpApplication
{
class Pentagon: Shape
    {
public Pentagon (string name)
            {
                    this.name = name;
```

```
                }

        public override void DisplayName()
            {
                Console.WriteLine ("This  is  a  child
class named: " + name);
            }
        }
}


}
```

Program Class

```
using System;

namespaceMyCSharpApplication
{
class Program
    {
static void Main(string[] args)
        {

            Shape s = new Shape();
            s.name = "Shape";
s.DisplayName();

            s = new Triangle("Triangle");
s.DisplayName();

            s = new Pentagon("Pentagon");
s.DisplayName();

Console.Read();
        }
    }
}
```

Chapter 9: Events and Delegates

In this chapter, we are going to study two very important concepts in C#: Delegates and Events. C#'s entire event handling mechanism is based on these two concepts. Delegates in C# are function pointers. They hold reference to a function. They provide decoupling between the calling function and the function being called. An event in C# is also a type of delegate. Events are used to invoke methods. For instance, when you click a button, an event fires which invokes all the methods associated with the event. In this chapter, we shall see these concepts in action.

Contents

- **Delegates**
- **Events**

1- Delegates

Delegates are classes which invoke a method which is passed to its constructor. Delegates store references to the method which is passed to it as a delegate. The first example of this chapter demonstrates how a delegate is created and how it is used to reference a method.

Example1:

```
using System;

namespaceMyCSharpApplication
{

public delegate intChangeIt(intnum);

class Program
    {
static void Main(string[] args)
        {

ChangeIt c = square;
Console.WriteLine("The square of 4 is: "+ c(4));

Console.Read();
        }

public static int square(intnum)
        {
returnnum * num;
        }
    }
}
```

In Example1, we created a delegate, "ChangeIt", by using the keyword "delegate". A delegate can only store references to methods that exactly match the signature of the delegate. For instance, in Example 1, the delegate signature is "intChangeit (intnum)". This means that this delegate can call any method which

85

accepts an integer type variable as a parameter and returns an integer type variable. In the "Program" class, we created a static method called "square". The signature of this method matches the signature of the "ChangeIt" delegate. Inside the "Main" method, we create a variable, "c", of the delegate "ChangeIt" and assign it the method "square". To invoke the method, we simply pass the parameter to variable "c". For instance, if we pass 4 to variable "c", the value returned would be 16 because, internally, "c" would call the "square" method. We then display the returned value on the screen.

Output1:

```
The square of 4 is: 16
```

2- Events

Events are also a type of delegate; however, during declaration, the keyword "event" is appended before the delegate name. Like delegates, events are also hooked to methods. Events can execute methods with a signature similar to the signature of the delegate type of the event. When the event is fired, one or more methods can be executed. Example2 demonstrates how events are hooked to methods and how these methods are called when an event is fired.

Example2:

```
using System;

namespaceMyCSharpApplication
{

public delegate void DisplayNameHandler();
```

```
class Program
    {
public static event DisplayNameHandlerNameChanged;
static void Main(string[] args)
        {

NameChanged += DisplayFruit;
NameChanged += DisplayAnimal;
NameChanged += DisplayFlower;
NameChanged += DisplayColor;

NameChanged.Invoke();

Console.Read();
        }

public static void DisplayFruit()
        {
Console.WriteLine("This is an apple.");
        }

public static void DisplayAnimal()
        {
Console.WriteLine("This is a lion.");
        }

public static void DisplayFlower()
        {
Console.WriteLine("This is a rose.");
        }

public static void DisplayColor()
        {
Console.WriteLine("This is red.");
        }
```

```
        }
    }
```

In Example 2, we created a delegate named "DisplayNameHandler". Inside the "Program" class, we created an event "NameChanged" of the delegate type "DisplayNameHandler". We declared four methods: "DisplayFruit", "DisplayAnimal", "DisplayFlower", and "DisplayColor". The signature of these methods is similar to the "DisplayNameHandler"; therefore, we can hook these four methods to the "NameChanged" event. To hook a method with any event, we simply add that method to the event name. In Example 1, the statement "NameChanged += DisplayFruit" depicts the hooking of method "DisplayFruit" to the "NameChanged" event. To fire an event, we simply call the "Invoke" method on that event. "Invoke" executes all the methods hooked with the "NameChanged" event in the order in which they are hooked. The output of the code in Example2 is as follows.

Output2:

```
This is an apple.
This is a lion.
This is a rose.
This is red.
```

Exercise 9

Task:

Create a delegate named "Calculations" which accepts two integer type parameters and returns one integer type value. In the "Program" class, create two methods, "sum" and "subtract", which have the same signature as the "Calculations" delegate. Create an object of the "Calculation" delegate and hook both the "sum" and "subtract" methods to it. Perform "sum" and "subtraction" on two random integers using the object of "Calculation" delegate hooked to the "sum" and "subtract" methods.

Solution

```
using System;

namespaceMyCSharpApplication
{

public delegate int Calculations(int num1, int num2);

class Program
    {

static void Main(string[] args)
        {

            Calculations c = Sum;

c(10, 5);

Console.WriteLine(c(10, 5));

            c += Subtract;
```

```
Console.WriteLine(c(10, 5));

Console.Read();
        }

public static int Sum(int num1, int num2)
        {
return num1 + num2;
        }

public static int Subtract (int num1, int num2)
        {
return num1 - num2;
        }

    }
}
```

Chapter 10: Multithreading

Up until this point, we have been working with single-threaded applications where program follow a single path of execution and only a single piece of code is executed at a particular time. This approach is suited to simple console based applications. However, in case of advanced GUI based applications, a single-threaded execution causes unresponsiveness and delayed execution. Consider a Windows form application where data has to be fetched before being displayed on the form. During the period when data is being fetched by the application, the user can do nothing on the front end of the form. If the database is huge, more time is spent fetching the data causing the front end of the application to behave unresponsively. Multithreading is the solution to such problems. In this chapter, we are going to study how to create threads and how they work together resulting in asynchronous program execution.

Contents

- **What is a thread?**
- **Thread Creation in C#**

- **Thread Join and Sleep**

1- What is a thread?

A thread is the smallest unit of execution. A thread runs inside a process. A process reserves operating system resources along with an exclusive execution environment. One process can have one or more threads. In single-threaded applications, only one thread runs inside a process, having exclusive access to all the process resources and the execution environment. In case of multithreaded applications, multiple threads run inside a process and they share several process resources, particularly memory and the execution environment. This sharing of resources leads to the solution of the unresponsiveness problem explained in the introduction. In multithreaded applications, one thread can fetch data from the database and store it in the shared memory, and the second thread can simultaneously display the fetched data on the front end of the application.

2- Thread Creation in C#

Creating a thread in C# is an extremely straight forward process. You just have to create an object of the "Thread". In the "Thread" class constructor, pass the method delegate that you want to run in a separate thread. Next, simply call the "Start" method on the object which you created. The first example of this chapter demonstrates thread creation and the execution process in detail. Have a look at it.

Example1:

```
using System;
usingSystem.Threading;
```

```
namespaceMyCSharpApplication
{
class Program
    {
static void Main(string[] args)
        {
                Thread t1 = new Thread(DisplayTwo);
                Thread t2 = new Thread(DisplayThree);

t1.Start();
t2.Start();

for (inti = 0; i< 100; i++)
                {
Console.Write("1");
                }
Console.Read();
        }

static void DisplayTwo()
        {
for (inti = 0; i< 100; i++)
                {
Console.Write("2");
                }
        }
static void DisplayThree()
        {
for (inti = 0; i< 100; i++)
                {
Console.Write("3");
                }
        }
    }
}
```

To perform threading related tasks in your program, you need to import "System" and "System.Threading" namespace in your code. C# runtime creates one thread by default for every program. This is the thread in which the "Main" method runs. In Example2, inside the "Main" method, we have created two objects of "Thread" class. These objects have been named t1, and t2. In the constructor of the first object, t1, we passed the "DisplayTwo" method delegate. This method displays the digit "2" one hundred times on console. This method has been defined immediately after the "Main". Similarly, in the constructor of the t2 object, the "DisplayThree" method has been called. This method displays the digit "3" one hundred times on the screen. After initializing t1 and t2 inside the "Main" method, the "Start" method has been called on this object. Calling "Start" on the thread object creates a new path of execution which runs parallel to already-executing threads. At this point in time, three threads are running simultaneously: The main thread (which is running the "Main" method) and the t1 and t2 threads (which are running "DisplayTwo" and "DisplayThree" methods). This means that now we have three execution paths which are being executed simultaneously. These three paths are simultaneously trying to print the digits "1", "2", and "3" on the screen, one hundred times each. The output of the code in Example1 is as follows:

Output1

```
3212312313131321333322123121332231223322132231211 2121
2131313111121223331231231323232122321212332231123321
331231223213223121132321223123322121211131321213 12332
2132133223122332132223131222233123322123313212331 2121
2311123212221313233211322312233213322123321232212 2133
31311313131313313331311111111111111
```

On the console screen, you will see that these digits are printed in a random order, although we called the "DisplayTwo" method first and then "DisplayThree". This is because all the threads are simultaneously trying to access the output console and print their respective digit; since control can only be accessed by one thread a time, it is randomly being allotted to each thread, resulting in a random display of digits on the output screen.

3- Thread Join and Sleep

In the previous section, we studied how multiple threads execute simultaneously. What if you want to let one thread complete its execution before proceeding further? To wait for an object to complete its execution, you call the "Join" method on that object. Similarly, if you want to stop thread execution for a particular time period, you can call the "Sleep" method on the thread class. This method takes times in milliseconds, or "TimeSpan" object, as its parameter.

To see this concept in action, have a look at the second example.

Example2:

```
using System;
usingSystem.Threading;

namespaceMyCSharpApplication
{
class Program
    {
static void Main(string[] args)
        {
            Thread t1 = new Thread(DisplayTwo);

t1.Start();

t1.Join();
```

```
Console.WriteLine("\n====================================
===========");
for (inti = 0; i< 100; i++)
                {
Console.Write("1");
if (i+1 == 50)
                        {
Console.WriteLine("\nThread    Sleeps    here    for    5
seconds...");
Thread.Sleep(5000);
                        }
                }
Console.Read();
        }

static void DisplayTwo()
        {
for (inti = 0; i< 100; i++)
                {
Console.Write("2");
                }
        }
    }
}
```

In Example2, we created thread object t1 which runs the "DisplayTwo" method. We start the thread execution by calling "Start" on this object. Immediately after calling "Start", we called "Join" on the t1 object in the next line. At this point, the thread inside which "Join" is called waits for the completion of the thread on which "Join" is called. This means that the "Main" method will wait for the complete execution of the t1 thread before executing itself further. After the t1 thread executes, the "Main" method will execute and the "for loop", which prints the digit "1", will also execute. When the "for loop" is executed 50 times, we call "Sleep" for 5 seconds. (5000 ms = 5 sec). The thread takes a break for 5 seconds and then prints the remaining digits. The output of the code in Example2 is as follows:

Output2:

```
222222222222222222222222222222222222222222222222222222
2222222222222222222222222222222222222222222222
==============================================
1111111111111111111111111111111111111111111111111
Thread Sleeps here for 5 seconds...
1111111111111111111111111111111111111111111111111
```

Exercise 10

Task:

Create two threads inside the "Main" method. One thread should call a method which displays "+" on console one hundred times. The other method should display "X" on the screen one hundred times. The "Main" method should wait for the completion of both of these threads, and then it should display "#" on the screen 20 times. It should then wait for 3 seconds before displaying "#" again, this time 60 times. Finally, it should wait for 3 more seconds before displaying "#" 20 more times.

Solution

```
using System;
usingSystem.Threading;
```

```csharp
namespaceMyCSharpApplication
{
class Program
    {
static void Main(string[] args)
        {
            Thread t1 = new Thread(DisplayPlus);
            Thread t2 = new Thread(DisplayMultiply);

t1.Start();
t2.Start();

t1.Join();
t2.Join();

Console.WriteLine("\n====================================
==========");
for (inti = 0; i< 100; i++)
            {
Console.Write("+");
if (i+1 == 20)
                {
Console.WriteLine("\nThread    Sleeps    here    for    3
seconds...");
Thread.Sleep(3000);
                }
if (i + 1 == 80)
                {
Console.WriteLine("\nThread    Sleeps    here    for    3
seconds...");
Thread.Sleep(3000);
                }

            }
Console.Read();
        }
```

```
static void DisplayPlus()
        {
for (inti = 0; i< 100; i++)
            {
Console.Write("+");
            }
        }

static void DisplayMultiply()
        {
for (inti = 0; i< 100; i++)
            {
Console.Write("X");
            }
        }
    }
}
```

Intermediate C# Programming

Welcome to the Intermediate C# Programming. In the next section, we'll start covering some advanced C# topics. Starting with the all important exception handling, this section will take you through Generics, Expression trees, and will end with LINQ (Language Integrated Query) after covering Null-able and Anonymous types.

Each chapter starts with a thorough summary of the topic and introduces the contents to be covered in the chapter. Sample code snippets with text and examples at end of each chapter (in the form of an exercise) are provided to ensure that you grasp each topic easily and comprehensively.

Chapter 11: Exception Handling

Exceptions are run time errors. That is, they arise during program execution, and are mostly an outcome of poor programming logic, i.e. division by zero, but not always.

While it is easy to detect and handle syntax or compile time errors in your code, since most compilers do that for you, logical errors (or exceptions) may or may not always be easy to foresee and manage. For example, in a simple program that takes user input, if the input type (as specified by programmer) is "int" but a user enters "string," an exception will occur, which if not already handled might result in an abrupt closure/stoppage of the application.

Exceptions like one above can be thought of beforehand, and are manageable to a large extent. However consider a case where you receive a memory buffer overflow, I/O file error, or database error. Errors like these and many others cannot always be predicted and may result in a system throwing exceptions.

In this chapter, you will see how you can manage exceptions occurring in your applications using the C# exception handling mechanism. This involves:

Contents

- **Try/Catch construct**
- **Finally keyword**
- **Throw keyword**

But before we see how we can manage exceptions occurring in our code, it's important that we know a few basic things about them. For instance, Exceptions are thrown by the "System.Exception" class and they are actually good in the sense that they save system failures. Hence, to write efficient code, it's imperative that we care for and handle exceptions that may occur in our programs ourselves. Let's now see how.

3- Try/Catch Construct

Working in tandem, a try/catch construct is mostly used to handle exceptions that may occur during run time. Putting our code in a "try { }" block saves our programs from abrupt closure. Inside the try block, if an exception occurs, the system instead of halting program execution, stops at the line where the error has occurred, and looks for a related "catch" block to transfer control by throwing occurred exceptions there. The catch block, as the name indicates, catches that exception, and does as per program instructions in that block.

The Basic Skelton of a try/catch block inside any program is:

```
try
{
    //Program Code that might raise an exception
}
```

```
catch
{
    //Exception gets handled inside
}
```

Let's see an example to better understand how it works.

Example 1:

```
using System;
using System.Collections;

namespace SampleApplication
{
    class Program
    {
        static void Main(string[] args)
        {
            int[] num = new int[2];

            num[0] = 13;
            num[1] = 22;
            num[2] = 42;
            foreach(int x in num)
            Console.WriteLine(x);
            Console.ReadLine();
        }
    }
}
```

If we try to execute the above code, we will receive an "Array out of Bound" exception, since our array size is 2 here while we are trying putting 3 objects in our array. But placing the above code in a try/catch block will result in a different outcome.

Example 2:

```
Int [] num = new int[2];
try
{
    num[0] = 13;
    num[1] = 22;
    num[2] = 42;

    foreach(int x in num)
        Console.WriteLine(x);
}
catch (Exception e)
{
  Console.WriteLine ('Error occurred: ' + e.Message);
}
Console.ReadLine();
        }
    }
}
```

Now, when we execute our code, the try {} block saves our program from throwing exceptions towards us, and instead passes it to our catch block. The catch block receives that exception in object "e" and simply displays the exception message on screen for us.

4- Finally keyword:

The code inside a "finally" block guarantees essential execution, irrespective of whether an exception occurs or not, or what type of exception occurs. Mostly, programmers use this block to print "ending" messages before closure in games or to close file references and garbage objects, as those are no longer required.

Another important thing to note here is that we can use multiple catch segments with the same try block. That is, each catch block can be used as a dedicated basket to catch only a unique type of exception and not all. This is quite useful if we want our program to do different things on each type of exception. To do that on the same code, we get:

Example 3:

```
public void F1()
    { Console.WriteLine('Control inside f1' );}
public void F2()
    { Console.WriteLine('Control inside f2' );}

Int [] num = new int[2];
try
{
    num[0] = 13;
    num[1] = 22;
    num[2] = 42;

    foreach(int x in num)
        Console.WriteLine(x);
}
catch(IndexOutOfRangeException e)
{
  Console.WriteLine('Index out of range found!');
F1();
}
catch(Exception e)
{
 Console.WriteLine('Some sort of error occured: ' +
e.GetType().ToString();
F2();
}
finally
{
```

```
Console.WriteLine('It's the end of our try code
block. Time to Sleep!');
}
```

Now, in the code above, if an "array out of bound" exception occurs during execution, the control or the exception is received by our first catch block that prints "Index out of range found!" and then calls F1(). However, if another exception occurs, e.g. buffer overflow for instance, the control will pass to our second catch block that will print out exception type by using the "e.GetType().ToString()" function and will call F2(). In both cases, the control will eventually be passed on to the "finally" segment.

5- Throw Keyword

If we are using the "throw" keyword in our programs, that only means that we are creating and throwing custom exceptions. The idea of creating and throwing exceptions ourselves sounds absurd at first, but it's actually more than handy to begin with. For instance, it's handy when you would like to transfer control if your program fails to open a target file, or is waiting for too long for an I/O resource, etc.

Example 4:

```
static void Main()
{
Try{
//your code
    Exception ex = new Exception ('The file was found
missing');
    throw e;
}}
catch (Exception e)
```

```
{Console.WriteLine (e.Message);}
}
```

Here for instance, if our code is looking for a file that it couldn't find it will create an exception object and will pass the control to a catch block using the throw keyword. We can then print out the exception on the console or do whatever our program requires.

Exercise 11

Task:

Create a custom exception if a user tries to divide a number by zero.

Solution

```
using System;
using System.Collections.Generic;
using System.ComponentModel;
namespace SampleApplication
{

    class Program
    {
        static void Main(string[] args)
        {

{
  try
  {
                int a = 0;
```

```
                int b = 10;
                int c = 0;
                c = b / a;
            }
        catch (Exception ex)
        {
                throw    (new    MyCustomException('You
cannot divide a number by 0'));
        }
        }
    }
    public class MyCustomException : System.Exception
    {
            public MyCustomException() : base() {}
            public MyCustomException(string message):
base(message)
            {
                MessageBox.Show(message);
            }
    }
}
```

Chapter 12: Lambda Expression and Expression Trees

In this chapter, we are going to study two new related features in the newest version of C# 3.0 and the .NET 3.0 runtime: Lambda expressions and Expression trees. We will learn how to create and use them to enhance and simplify our C# code. The knowledge behind the concept of delegates which we have already studied in *C# Programming for Beginners* will be useful for the understanding of this chapter.

Contents

- **Lambda Expressions.**
- **Expression Trees.**

4- Lambda Expressions

A Lambda Expression is an anonymous function that is used to create delegates or expression tree types. Lambda Expressions give us a fast and easy way to define delegates. A Lambda Expression is like a method without a declaration, i.e. access modifiers. The usage of Lambda Expressions can save you two or three lines of code per call. It speeds up your application development and makes the code maintainable and reusable.

It also allows us to write our methods exactly at the same place where we are going to use them. Lambda Expressions are similar to anonymous methods - just slightly smarter in syntax, but both compile to the same intermediate language.

Lambdas are also used in method-based LINQ queries (as you will see in the chapter on LINQ) as arguments to standard query operator methods such as "Where."

Lambda Expressions follow the basic signature:

Parameters => Executed code

Example 1:

```
y =>    y*y;
```

In the above example, "y" is the input parameter, and "y*y" is the expression. The Lambda Expression specifies the parameter named '"y" and it returns the value of its square.

We can assign this Lambda Expression to a delegate like:

```
delegate int del(int i);
static void Main(string[] args){
del myDelegate = y => y * y;
 int resultVariable= myDelegate(8);
}
```

In the above example, we assign a Lambda Expression "y => y * y" to a delegate "myDelegate" and then call myDelegate with a value "8" and stores the result of this Lambda Expression in an integer variable "resultVariable" which is equal to 64.

Example 2:

```
Class LambdaExpression{
static void Main(string[] args){
List<string> names=new List<string>();
 names.Add('James');
 names.Add('Troy');
 names.Add('Harry');
 string
resultString=names.Find(name=>name.Equals('Troy'));
}
}
```

In the above example, we declare a List of String values "names" then add different names to this list with the built-in function "list.Add". Next we can find a specific name with the built-in function "list.Find" and pass a Lambda Expression "name=>name.Equals('Troy')" to this built-in function which saves the required result to a string literal named "resultString".

Example 3:

```
namespace lambdaexample

{
```

```
class QueryOperator

{

  static void Main(string[] args)

  {

    int[] numbers = { 1, 1, 2, 3, 5, 8, 13, 21, 34 };

    double averageNumber = numbers.Where(num => num % 2 ==
1).Average();

    Console.WriteLine(averageNumber);

    Console.ReadLine();

  }

}

}
```

In the above example, we declare an array of integers "numbers" which holds Fibonacci numbers, and we use the Lambda Expression with a where clause "numbers.Where(num => num % 2 == 1).Average()". The part "num => num % 2 == 1" of the expression is getting the odd numbers from the list, and then retrieving their average with the built-in function "Average ()" and then saving it to a double type variable "averageNumber". Lastly, it prints the result on the console by using this statement Console.WriteLine(averageNumber).

5- Expression Trees

A data structure that contains Expressions such as Lambda Expressions is known as an Expression tree. As Expressions are pieces of code, to put it simply, they are a tree structure with pieces of code in them, and can be executed by running the Lambda Expression over a set of data. Generally speaking, expression trees are a kind of Binary tree because by using binary trees you can quickly find the data you need. Expression trees provide us a method to translate the executable code into data. You can use it to transform the C# code. For example, LINQ query expression code can be transformed to operate on another SQL database process.

Example 4:

```
Func <int, int, int> function = (a, b) => a + b;
```

The above statement has three parts:

- A declaration: Func<int,int,int> function
- An equals operator: =
- A Lambda Expression: (a,b) => a+b;

The variable "function" is the executable code which can hold the result obtained from a Lambda Expression ((a,b) => a+b). Now you can call the Lambda Expression like this:

```
int c = function(5, 5);
```

When we call the function, the variable c will be set equal to 5+5, which is 10.

Since expression trees are a form of a data structure you can convert this executable code into a data structure by using a simple syntax of LINQ. You have to add the Linq.Expressions namespace in order to achieve this.

```
using System.Linq.Expressions;
```

Next, create the expression tree like this:

```
Expression<Func<int, int, int>> expression = (a,b) =>
a + b;
```

Now the above mentioned Lambda Expression is converted into an expression tree such as "Expression<X>". The identifier expression is not executable code; it is a data structure called an expression tree.

In Visual Studio (IDE), you can see the expression tree of the expression statement in a program "ExpressionTreeVisualizer".

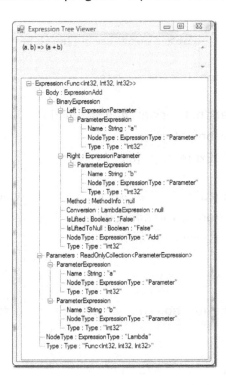

In the above diagram, you can see the Lambda Expression and its constituent part in TreeView Control.

In the above example, there are four properties in the Expression<x> class:

- Body
- Parameters
- NodeType
- Type

If we collapse the nodes of the tree shown as in the above diagram, the four properties will be clearly visible.

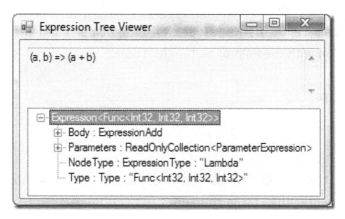

```
BinaryExpression body =
(BinaryExpression)expression.Body;
ParameterExpression left =
(ParameterExpression)body.Left;
ParameterExpression right =
(ParameterExpression)body.Right;
Console.WriteLine(expression.Body);
Console.WriteLine(' The left part of the expression:
' +
   '{0}{4} The NodeType: {1}{4} The right part: {2}{4}
The Type: {3}{4}',
   left.Name, body.NodeType, right.Name, body.Type,
Environment.NewLine);
```

From the above lines of code, we can easily explore the expression tree. Let's see now how the code works. First, you are declaring the variable "body" of type "BinaryExpression" which holds the body of the expression. In this example it is (a+b). Then, we extract the left parameter of the body with (ParameterExpression)body.Left" in a variable "left" of the type "parameterExpression." In this case it is the variable "a." Next, we are extracting the right parameter of the body with "(ParameterExpression)body.Right" in a variable "right" of the type "parameterExpression" which in our case is the variable "b". Next, we are simply printing the body of the expression to the console as well as its NodeType, left & right part, and the type of expression with the help of built-in functions.

Exercise 12

Task 1:

Write a Lambda Expression which calculates the total number of scores greater than 60 in this series (91, 73, 84, 97, 75, 65, 40, and 89).

Solution

```
class SampleLambda
{
    static void Main()
    {
        int[] scores = { 91, 73, 84, 97, 75, 65, 40,
89};

        int highScores = scores.Where(n => n >
60).Count();

        Console.WriteLine('{0} scores are greater
than 80', highScores);
```

```
    }
}
```

Task 2:

Create the query which retrieves the total scores for First grade Students, Second grade, and so on using Lambda Expression.

Solution

```
private static void StudentsByGrade()
{
    var categ =
    from student in students
    group student by student.grade into studentGroup
    select new   {   GradeLevel   =   studentGroup.Key,
TotalScore      =         studentGroup.Sum(s           =>
s.ExamScores.Sum()) };

    foreach (var cat in categ)
    {
        Console.WriteLine ('Key  =  {0}  Sum  =  {1}',
cat.GradeLevel, cat.TotalScore);
    }
}
```

Chapter 13: Generics

In <u>C# Programming for Beginners</u>, we were introduced to arrays. By now, most of us are well familiar with defining and using arrays in our programs. However, the problem with arrays is this: you have to define them "explicitly" before you can use them. That is, their data type, their size, etc, have to be defined before you use them.

Generics, on the other hand, are flexible, moldable, and efficient. With Generics, you don't have to specify the data type of a list, class, or method beforehand. In other words, they allow us to create strongly typed/type-safe data structures without specifying the exact data types at the time of their declaration. That means you can write "type less" classes, functions, and container lists. This is also their biggest advantage, since you can now create one class or method, and can use it over and over, each time with a different data type.

In this chapter, we will discuss Generics in depth.

Contents

i.   **Generics List <T> Collection**

Generic collections (Lists) allow you to create data types that have the functionalities of both Arrays and Array Lists. From their signature and usage, they are just like Arrays. You declare them, initialize their members, and then use them. Let's see how.

Example 1:

```
using System;

namespace MySampleApplication
{
    class Program
    {
        static void Main(string[] args)
        {
Int x=0;
            List<int> myRows = new List <int> ();
                myRows.Add(1);
                myRows.Add(2);
                myRows.Add(3);
            While (x<myRows.Count)
{
     Console.WriteLine('Generics :{0}', myRows[x]);
++x;
}
        }
    }
}
```

Before diving into what the above code does, let's first have a basic understanding of few things: First let's look at Generic List<int> "myRows". Notice here that the type signature of a List class is List <T> where T can be any data type. It can be int, string, char, or any custom defined type. A List of type string will only hold strings, a list of custom defined type Bicycle will only occupy Bicycle objects (strictly typed). Hence our List myRows here will only occupy objects of type int.

The other thing to note here is the Add() function. Using myRows.Add(), you can define as many "int" entities in the list as you would like, unlike arrays where we have to specify the size in their definition. Add() however isn't the only method that we can use with List <T> objects. There are numerous others including Contains, Remove, etc.

While Arrays have their length property that tells us their size, List <T> has the "Count" property that does the same thing.

The output of Example 1 is shown as follows:

Output 1:

```
Generics :{ 1} Generics :{ 2} Generics :{ 3}
```

The code works like this: We have declared a List myRows of type int. Using the Add method, we add three entities of value 1, 2, and 3. Then, using a while loop we print their values on the console using List's Count Property.

ii.   Generic Methods

Generic methods, as well as generic classes, allow us to reuse our code in many different ways. Declaring and using a generic method that uses data types as parameters is both easy and fun to work do.

120

While generic methods are mostly added into existing generic classes, they are equally handy where containing classes are not generic or where a method contains parameters that were not initially defined for the generic class parameters. Generic methods follow the basic pattern of "method name (type param syntax)". Consider the following code, for instance:

Example 2:

```
namespace MySampleApplication
{
 public static class MathExp
{
   public static T Max<T>(T first, params T[] values)
       where T : IComparable
   {
       T max = first;
       foreach (T item in values)
       {
           if (item.CompareTo(max) > 0)
           {max = item;   }
       }
       return max;
   }
   public static T Min<T>(T first, params T[] values)
       where T : IComparable
   {
       T mini = first;
        foreach (T item in values)
     {
       if (item.CompareTo(mini) < 0)
            { mini = item;  }
        }
       return mini;
   }
}
```

The sample class "MathExp" has two generic methods: "Min <T> and Max <T>". The functionality of both functions is quite simple. Given a list of values, Min<T> will find and return the minimum value from the list passed as a parameter, while the Max<T> will output the maximum or greatest value among the parameters. The syntax "<T>" simply refers to the fact that we can use both of these methods with any type of data values, i.e. int, strings, etc.

Consider now that we call our Max<T> function with int values first e.g., Console.WriteLine (MathEx.Max<int> (6, 56, 760)) and then with string type values e.g. (Console.WriteLine (MathEx.Max<string> ("Apple," "Banana," "Pineapple")). Our output will be:

Output 2:

```
760
Pineapple
```

Note that we have specified the type of data values that we are passing in both cases above, i.e. <int> and <string>. It's fine to call generic methods this way, as long as it's for our own clarity. However, the C# compiler does not need that, since it can infer the data types itself while compiling which is also known as "type interfacing." To see "Type interfacing" at work, let's again call the above methods, this time without explicitly specifying their data types by using Console.WriteLine (MathEx.Max (6, 56, 760)) and Console.WriteLine (MathEx.Max ("Apple","Banana","Pineapple")). It should be no surprise that our output will be the same as before.

Output 3:

```
760
```

However, it's important to know here that type interfacing won't work, and in fact will result in a compile type error if we were to call the same function with a call like "MathEx.Max(7.0, 49)" with multiple value types, such as int and float. For type interfacing to work, all the parameter values must obey the defined method signature.

Exercise 13

Task:

Create a generic swap function.

Solution

```csharp
using System;
using System.Collections.Generic;

namespace GenericSwapSolution
{
    class Program
    {
        static void SwapIt<T>(ref T left, ref T right)
        {
            T tmp;
            tmp = left;
            left = right;
            right = tmp;
        }
        static void Main(string[] args)
        {
```

```
        int x, y;
        char a, b;
        x = 20; y = 40;
        a = 'G'; b = 'I';
 Console.WriteLine('Int values before swap are:');
 Console.WriteLine('x = {0}, y = {1}', x, y);
Console.WriteLine('Char values before swap are:');
  Console.WriteLine('a = {0}, b = {1}', a, b);

        Swap<int> (ref x, ref y);
        Swap<char> (ref a, ref b);

Console.WriteLine('Int values after swap are:');
Console.WriteLine('x = {0}, y = {1}', x, y);
Console.WriteLine('Char values after swap are:');
  Console.WriteLine('a = {0}, b = {1}', a, b);
        Console.ReadKey();
    }
  }
}
```

Chapter 14: Extension Methods

Extension Methods (introduced in C# 3.0) provides programmers with a simple framework to "extend" the functionalities of existing types in their programs. "Static" in nature, Extension Methods gives you the freedom to add already present methods into your types without a need to create new derived types or modifying old ones. They use a "this" keyword in their parameters / parameters lists. Since they are "static" methods, it's essential for you to use them in static classes. However, they are used as if they were instance methods of the extended type.

In this chapter, we will discuss Extension Methods in depth, and will learn:

Contents

- **What Extension Methods are**
- **How to create them**
- **How to applying Extension Methods to existing types**

i.   Extension Methods

The OCP, Open close principle, directs programmers to write code and functions in a way that they are open for extension all the time, but dead end on modification. In C#, Extension Methods are a practical case of OCP, which we can use in both custom defined and system defined user types to cater to our requirements.

It's also important for us to know a few basic facts about Extension Methods and how they work. One, they have only access (and hence can only use) the "public" properties of the data type they are extending. Two, their type signature should never be the same as any existing method of that type. Three, to use Extension Methods, their parent type must be in the namespace of the calling application. Four, in the case of a method overloading (methods with same signature), an instance method will be executed (called) instead of the Extended Method (as per the overload resolution mechanism), and lastly, we cannot apply Extension Methods on events, properties, and fields.

Before the addition of these methods, the common practice was to create custom types based on generic/primitive data types. With their addition however, we can now add functionalities to existing classes and functions without tampering with the code type. Let's consider a simple example where we are looking to provide the negative of a variable. The generic, or old way, of doing that is:

Example 1:

```
struct MyExample
{
    int num;

    public MyExample(int val)
```

```
    {
        this.num = val;
    }

    public int Negative()
    {
        return -num;
    }
}

static void Main(string[] args)
{

    MyExample i = new MyInt(34);
    Console.WriteLine(i.Negative());
}
```

While the code is quite basic, where we have created a strict "MyExample()" that has a simple function that returns negative of our passed value.

ii. Creating Extension Methods

The code above works fine, but technically speaking we are not actually extending the type of our existing type. Instead we have created a new type altogether. Hence, if we are really looking to "extend" the functionality of our existing type, we should be doing something better and more generic than that.

Example 2:

```
static class MySampleExtension
{
    public static int Negative(this int val)
    {
```

```
        return -val;
    }
}

static void Main(string[] args)
{

    int i = 53;
    Console.WriteLine(i.Negative());
}
```

While the basic functionality and output of this is similar in that it will output the negative of the passed "int", how it works is different. See the method declaration here: "public static int Negative()". We are adding our method "negative" with type "int" and are bounding it to be called only with the int type. We are not creating a new type as in the previous example, and we are only extending functionality of the type "int". Hence, to create our Extension Methods, we should:

- Have a "Static" class.
- Use a "public static" method with the same name as the class and have an explicit return type.
- Use the parameters type with the "this" keyword.

The "this" keyword is very important since it tells our compiler that we are "extending" this type and are not using it as an expected argument type.

iii.   Extension Methods on existing types

Using the above created Extension Method, let's now see how we can call an Extension Method on our existing types. Also note that we used the "this" keyword above, but what about the cases where we want to use additional parameters? We can easily do this too by defining all such parameters with their expected data type after specifying our "extending" type with the "this" keyword. The code below will help us to better understand:

Example 3:

```
static class MySampleExtMethods
{
    public static int Negative(this int val)
    {
        return -val;
    }

    public static int Multiply(this int val, int multi)
    {
        return val * multi;
    }
}

static void Main(string[] args)
{
    int i = 8;
    Console.WriteLine(' Using Extension method the input yields: {0}', i.Multiply(2));
}
```

Note that here we have defined another extension function called "Multiply". While we are extending it on type "int" as specified by "this in val", the second argument "int multi" lacks the "this" keyword. This is because we are using the second argument as an "argument," and extending it with the first type. However, note that we can also pass "strings," "char," or "float" values in "arguments" as our needs warrant.

The rest of the code is quite straightforward. We have created two extension methods and are calling the "multiply" method with such an argument of "2," and are extending it on the value of "I" which is 8. The output of above code will be:

Output 3:

```
16
```

Exercise 14

Task:

Create an Extension Method that checks if a string is an int or not, and if it is, convert the string's numeric value into a corresponding int value. For example, string str="2345" should be converted into int or return false otherwise.

Solution

```
using System;
using System.Text;

namespace SampleExtensionMethod
{
    public static class SampleClass
    {
public static bool IsInt(this string x)
    {
        float outcome;
        return float.TryParse(x, out outcome);
    }

  public static int IntExt(this string str)
```

```
        {
            return Int32.Parse(str);
        }
    }
    class Caller
    {
    static void Main (string [] args)
        {
 string str= '2345';
if (str.IsInt())
    { Console.WriteLine('Yes It's an integer');
 int nmb=str.IntExt();
     Console.WriteLine('The output using our custom
Integer extension method: {0}', nmb); }
else
    Console.WriteLine('No, it's not an integer.');

        Console.ReadLine();
        }
    }
}
```

Chapter 15 Nullable Types

C# provides some special types that consist of an additional null value along with the usual possible range of values of that data type. For example, an int32 data type can store a value ranging from -2147483648 to 2147483647 while the nullableint32 is able to store a null value along with its original possible range. Similarly, in the case of a Boolean variable, the Nullable of a Boolean variable is able to store a true, false, or a null value in it.

In this chapter we will study:

Contents

- **Structures of Nullable types in C#**
- **Syntax of Nullable types**
- **The HasValue and Has Property**
- **The Null Coalescing operator**

i. **Structures of Nullable types in C#**

The following table demonstrates the Nullable structure of a primitive data type along with the range of data that each data type can store. Nullable types have an additional value of Null.

Type	Range
Nullable Boolean	True or False or Null
Nullable byte	0 to 255 or Null
Nullable decimal	(-7.9 x 1028 to 7.9 x 1028) / 100 to 28 or Null
Nullable double	(+/-)5.0 x 10-324 to (+/-)1.7 x 10308 or Null
Nullable DateTime	Represents an instant in Time or Null
Nullable Int16	-32,768 to +32,767 or Null
Nullable Int32	-2,147,483,648 to 2,147,483,647 or Null

Nullable Int64	-9,223,372,036,854,775,808 to +9,223,372,036,854,775,807 Or Null
Nullable Single	Single value or Null
Nullable char	U+0000 to U+FFFF or Null

ii. Syntax for Nullable types in C#

Nullable types can be declared in two ways. The Syntax for the first way to declare a Nullable type is as follows:

```
System.Nullable<data_type> <variable_name> ;
```

It starts with the System.Nullable keyword, followed by data_type (i.e., int, double) followed by the variable name.

The Syntax for declaring a Nullable type the other way is:

```
< data_type> ? <variable_name> = null;
```

Starting with the data_type (i.e., int, double), it is followed by a question mark and then the name of variable.

Let's now see Nullable types at work.

Example 1:

```
Namespace nullable
{
    Class program
```

```
{
    static void Main ()
    {
      int? a= null;
      int? b=10;
      if(a==null)
     {System.Console.WriteLine(b.Value)}
      else {System.Console.WriteLine('Undefined');}
      Console.readKey();
      }
   }
}
```

In the example above, we have declared two nullable integers a and b. int? a has a null value and int? b has a value of 10. The if/else construct is quite basic too; if "a" has a null value, the program will print out the value of int? b. Otherwise, it will print "undefined".

Output 1:

```
10
```

The following example illustrates the Nullable type in action for Boolean and DateTime types.

Example 2:

```
Namespace nullable
{
    Class program
    {
      static void Main ()
      {
```

```
        int? a= null;
        int? b=5;
        Double? c=null;
        Double? d=6
        bool? Val= new bool?();
        DateTime? Start= DateTime.today;
        DateTime? End= null;
Console.Writeline('Showing values of Nullables: {0}, {1}, {2},
{3}',a,b,c,d);
Console.Writeline('A Nullable Boolean Variable: {0}',Val);
Console.Writeline(Start);
Console.Writeline('We don't know yet:', End);

Console.readKey();
        }
    }
}
```

In this program, we are using the Nullables of int, double, Boolean, and DateTime. Later, we are simply displaying them on the console. As the program compiles, it shows the values of the variables as:

Output 2:

```
Showing values of Nullables:, 5, , 6
A Nullable Boolean Variable:
6/8/2015 12:00:00 AM
We don't know yet:
```

iii.   The HasValue and Value Property

The Nullable type instances have two properties. These are public and read-only properties.

- **HasValue Property:**

The HasValue always returns a Boolean value. It can be true or false. If the type contains an integer or a non-null value, the Hasvalue property is true. If the type doesn't have a value or it is null, the Hasvalue property is false.

- **Has Property:**

The value is of the same type as the declared type. The Has property has a value if the Hasvalue property is true. If the Hasvalue property is false, the Has property will throw an Exception. See the code below to better understand this:

Example 3:

```
using System;
Namespace nullable
{
    Class program
    {
      static void Main ()
      {
      int? a= null;
      Console.WriteLine(a.HasValue); // HasValue property is
false
      Console.WriteLine(a.Value);    // will cause an exception
      Console.readKey();
      }
    }
}
```

Because our variable "a" has a null value the "HasValue" property will be false. If we try to display the "Value" on the console, we get an exception.

Output 3:

```
False
```

Example 4:

```csharp
using System;
Namespace nullable
{
    Class program
    {
    static void Main ()
    {
    int? a= null;
    Console.WriteLine(a.HasValue); // HasValue property is
false

    a=5; //assigning value to variable
    Console.WriteLine(a.HasValue); // hasvalue Property is true
because a has non-null value
    Console.WriteLine(a.Value);     // returns value of a
    Console.WriteLine(a);

    Console.readKey();
    }
 }
```

Output 4:

```
False
True
5
```

iv.   The Null Coalescing Operator

C# provides an operator to check the Null values. If it finds a Null value variable, it assigns a value to that variable. It is denoted by double question mark (??). We can use this operator for both Nullable types and reference types. It converts an operand to the type of another value type operand if the implicit conversion is possible. Let's see how it works:

Example 5:

```
using System;
Namespace nullable
{
    Class program
    {
      static void Main ()
    {
      int? a= null;
      int? b=3;
      int c=a ?? 5;
      System.Console.WriteLine('Value of c is: {0}',c);
      C=b ?? 5;
      System.Console.WriteLine('Value of c is: {0}',c);
      Console.readKey();
      }
    }
}
```

Output 5:

```
Value of c is: 5
Value of c is: 3
```

Exercise 15

Task:

Write a program using a Nullable integer and double values implementing the HasValue property and the Null coalescing properties.

Solution:

```
using System;
using System.Collections.Generic;
using System.Linq;
using System.Text;
using System.Threading.Tasks;

namespace nullable
{
    class Program
    {
        static void Main(string[] args)
        {
            int? a = null;
            Console.WriteLine(a.HasValue);
                int? b=3;
                Double? d=null;
                Double? e = 4;
    int c=a ?? 6;
```

```
System.Console.WriteLine('Value of Int c when
assigned to null is: {0}',c);
  c=b ?? 6;
System.Console.WriteLine('Value of Int c
reassigning is: {0}',c);


  Double f = d ?? 8;
System.Console.WriteLine('Value of Double f when
assigned is:{0}', f);
  f = e ?? 8;
System.Console.WriteLine('Value of Double f
reassigning is: {0}', f);
                a = 1;      //assigning value to variable
                d = 2;      // aasigning value to variable
                Console.WriteLine(a.HasValue);
                Console.WriteLine(d.HasValue);
                Console.WriteLine(a.Value);
                Console.WriteLine(d.Value);
                Console.WriteLine(a);
                Console.WriteLine(d);

                Console.ReadKey();
            }
        }
}
```

Chapter 16: Anonymous Types

C# enables its users to create new data types. Anonymous types are data types that a user can create without defining them. These types are created at the point of instantiation. Anonymous types are both compiler generated and are reference types derived from objects. The compiler defines them itself on the basis of their properties (names, numbers, etc.). It is an important feature used in SQL like LINQ. Anonymous types are useful in LINQ queries because LINQ (language integrated query) is integrated into C#. In C#, the properties created for Anonymous types are read only. This concept was introduced in C# 3.

In this chapter, we will study "Anonymous" types including:

Contents

- **The Var Statement**
- **Creating and Using Anonymous types**
- **Comparing Two Anonymous Instances**

i. Var Statement:

It is a data type introduced in C# 3.0. The "Var" data type is used to declare the local variables implicitly. Let's have a look at a few valid Var statements.

```
var str='name';
var num='5';
var array=new[]{0,1,2};
```

Now look at how the compiler compiles these statements:

```
var str='name';       // string str='name';
var num='5'           // int num='5';
var array=new[]{0,1,2}; // int array=new[]{0,1,2};
```

Extending basic functionality, let's have a look at a simple code snippet:

Example 1:

```
Using System;
using System.Collections.Generic;
using System.Linq;
using System.Text;
using System.Threading.Tasks;

namespace anonymous

{
    class Program
    {

        static void Main(string[] args)

        {
            var name = 'Alberta johnson';
            var number = 15;
            string s = 'Canada';
            var s2 = s;
            s2 = null;
            string s3 = null;
```

```
            var s4 = s3;
            Console.WriteLine(name);
            Console.WriteLine(number);
            Console.WriteLine(s);
            Console.WriteLine(s2);
            Console.WriteLine(s3);
            Console.WriteLine(s4);
            Console.ReadKey();

        }

    }

}
```

Output 1:

```
Alberta johnson
15
Canada
```

The values of variables var s2, var s3, and var s4 are null. The value of a var variable cannot be Null at compile time but can be Null at run time.

These types' var name and var string are not anonymous types. Actually, we are not declaring the data types of the variable, and the var statement shows that the compiler is itself deciding their data types.

Other Invalid var statements:

```
var a;              // invalid because it need to be initialized
var num=null        // cannot be Null at compile time
var v='Lord Belish'
v=15                // an integer value cannot be assigned to a
string variable declared implicitly
```

ii.   **Creating and Using Anonymous types in C#**

In short, Anonymous types are reference types, and can be declared or created using the var statement using the same syntax as used for regular types. For example, if we need to create an Anonymous type to represent a point, we can do that simply:

```
Var point = new {x=17,y=9};
```

As we have discussed earlier, for var statements initialization is compulsory, and a variable cannot be initialized to null value.

```
Var point = new {x=null,y=9};   //wrong statement, cannot be null
at compile time
```

Example 2

```
namespace anonymous
{
    class Program
    {
        static void Main(string[] args)
        {
            var Name = new { FirstName = 'Albert', LastName =
'Camus' };
            Console.WriteLine(Name.Firstname);
            Console.WriteLine(Name.Lastname);
            Console.ReadKey();

        }

    }

}
```

Output 2:

```
Albert
Camus
```

Let's now see how the complier creates an anonymous type.

145

```
namespace anonymous
{
    class Program
    {
        static void Main(string[] args)
        {
            var Employee = new { EmpName = 'George', EmpAddress =
'Camus' , Empsalary='25,000'};


        }

    }
}
```

At compile time, the compiler will create an anonymous type as
follows:

```
namespace anonymous
{
    class Program
    {
private string Name;
private string Address;
int salary;

public string EmpName

{get {return EmpName;}

 Set {EmpName=value;}

}

Public string EmpAddress

{

Get{return EmpAddress;}

Set{EmpAddress=value;}
}

Public int Empsalary

{
```

```
Get{return Empsalary;}
set{Empsalary=value;}

} }

}
```

We are naming the properties explicitly in all examples. We can do it implicitly if they are set on the basis of a property, or field, or a variable.

Example 3:

```
namespace anonymous
{
    class Program
    {
        static void Main(string[] args)
        {
            int variable = 42;
            var implicitProperties = new { variable, DateTime.Now
};
            var explicitProperties = new { variable = variable,
Now = DateTime.Now }; //same

as above
            Console.WriteLine('Time is
'+implicitProperties.Now+'And implicit Variable is ' +
                              implicitProperties.variable);
            Console.WriteLine('Time is
'+explicitProperties.Now+'And Explicit Variable is ' +
                              explicitProperties.variable);


            Console.ReadKey();

        }

    }

}
```

Output 3:

```
Time is 6/9/2015 4:30:06PM And Implicit variable is
42
Time is 6/9/2015 4:30:06PM And Explicit variable is
42
```

iii.   Comparing Two Anonymous Instances:

Anonymous types creates overrides of "Equals()" based on the
underlying properties, so we can compare two anonymous
variables. We can also get their Hash Codes using "GetHashCode()".
For example, if we had the following 3 points:

Example 4:

```
namespace anonymous
{
    class Program
    {
        static void Main(string[] args)
        {
            var point1 = new { A = 1, B = 2 };
            var point2 = new { A = 1, B = 2 };
            var point3 = new { b = 2, A = 1 };
    Console.WriteLine(point1.Equals(point2));
            // true, equal anonymous type instances
always have same hash code
    Console.WriteLine(point1.GetHashCode() ==
point2.GetHashCode());
    Console.WriteLine(point2.Equals(point3));
            // quite possibly false
    Console.WriteLine(point2.GetHashCode() ==
point3.GetHashCode());
            Console.ReadKey();
        }
```

148

```
        }
}
```

Output 4:

```
True
True
False
False
```

Exercise 16

Task:

Write a program of an object collection having properties FirstName, LastName, DOB, and MiddleName. Return Firstname and LastName querying the data using Anonymous types.

Solution:

```
namespace anonymous
{
    class MyData
    {
    public string FirstName { get; set; }
    public string LastName { get; set; }
    public DateTime DOB { get; set; }
    public string MiddleName { get; set; }
        static void Main(string[] args)
        {

            List<MyData> data = new List<MyData>();
```

```csharp
    data.Add(new MyData { FirstName = 'Shelby', LastName =
'Frank', MiddleName = 'N', DOB = new DateTime(1990, 12, 30) });
    data.Add(new MyData { FirstName = 'sara', LastName =
'Simpson', MiddleName = 'G', DOB = new DateTime(1995, 11, 6) });
    data.Add(new MyData { FirstName = 'Abigaile', LastName =
'jhonson', MiddleName = 'G', DOB = new DateTime(1993, 10, 8) });
    data.Add(new MyData { FirstName = 'George', LastName =
'Kanes', MiddleName = 'P', DOB = new DateTime(1983, 6, 15) });
    data.Add(new MyData { FirstName = 'Alberto', LastName =
'Delrio', MiddleName = 'K', DOB = new DateTime(1988, 7, 20) });

    var anonymousData= from people in data
                    select new{people.FirstName, people.LastName};
        foreach(var n in
anonymousData){Console.WriteLine('Name: ' + n.FirstName+ ' ' +
n.LastName);}

    Console.ReadKey();
}


}
```

Chapter 17: LINQ part 1

LINQ is an acronym for "Language Integrated Query." Those familiar with databases will already know what a "query" is. A query is basically a programmer's way of interacting with a database for manipulating data. That is, using queries, programmers can access database tables in order to insert, edit, retrieve, or delete data. Unlike a traditional mechanism of querying data, LINQ provides C# developers with a completely new way to access and work with multiple types of data including XML files, databases, Lists, and dynamic data.

LINQ functions have two basic units: sequences and elements. A LINQ sequence is a set of items which implements the IEnumerable<T> interface. Each item in the set is called the element. A typical example of a collection that implements the IEnumerable<T> interface is the array collection. Have a look at the following string array:

```
string[] cities = {"Paris", "Washington", "Moscow",
"Athens", "London" };
```

Here, this string type array contains names of different cities. This type of collection is called a local sequence, because all the items in the collection are in the local memory of the system.

Query Operators

Query operators in LINQ are used to take a LINQ sequence as input, transform the sequence, and return the transformed sequence as output. The Enumerable class of the System.Linq namespace contains around 40 query operators. In the following section, we will show the workings of some of the most commonly used LINQ operators.

i-   Where operator

The "where" operator is used to filter a sequence based on a particular condition. For instance, if you want to get the name of all the cities in the "cities" array where length of the city is greater than or equal to 6, you can do so in the following manner.

Example1:

```
using System;
using System.Collections;
using System.Collections.Generic;
using System.Linq;
namespace MyCSharpApplication
{
    class Program
    {

        public static void Main()
```

```
        {

                string[] cities = {"Paris", "Washington",
"Moscow","Athens", "London" };

                List<string> citiesendingwiths = (from c in cities
                                         where c.Length
>=6
                                         select
c).ToList();

                foreach(string c in citiesendingwiths)
                {
                    Console.WriteLine(c);
                }

                Console.Read();
            }
        }

}
```

The sequence of a LINQ query is quite similar to that of SQL query. In Example1, we simply fetched all the cities with a length greater than or equal to 6, and then displayed it on the console screen. In this case, all the city names in the cities array will be displayed except "Paris," which is only 5 characters in lenght.

The LINQ syntax used in Example1 is commonly referred to as query syntax owing to its similarity to the SQL query syntax. However, there is another way to execute LINQ queries using Lambda Expressions. This is known as fluent syntax. Example 2 demonstrates how fluent syntax is used to achieve the same functionality of Example1.

Example 2

```csharp
using System;
using System.Collections;
using System.Collections.Generic;
using System.Linq;
namespace MyCSharpApplication
{
    class Program
    {

        public static void Main()
        {

            string[] cities = {"Paris", "Washington",
"Moscow","Athens", "London" };

            List<string>        citiesendingwiths        =
cities.Where(c => c.Length >= 6).ToList();

            foreach(string c in citiesendingwiths)
            {
                Console.WriteLine(c);
            }

            Console.Read();
        }
    }

}
```

Like SQL, logical operators can also be used along with comparison operators in LINQ. For instance, if you want to retrieve the names of all the cities which have a character length greater than 5 and have "o" in their names, you can use the AND logical operator as follows:

Example3:

```
using System;
using System.Collections;
using System.Collections.Generic;
using System.Linq;
namespace MyCSharpApplication
{
    class Program
    {

        public static void Main()
        {

            string[] cities = {"Paris", "Washington",
"Moscow","Athens", "London" };

            List<string>    citiesendingwiths    =
cities.Where(c    =>    c.Length    >=    6    &&
c.Contains("o")).ToList();

            foreach(string c in citiesendingwiths)
            {
                Console.WriteLine(c);
            }

            Console.Read();
        }
    }

}
```

This time, only the cities Washington, Moscow, and London will be displayed on the screen since these are the only cities having "o" in their names and a character length greater than or equal to 6.

2- Select

A Select query is mostly used with objects with multiple members. Select can be used to retrieve a particular member of all the objects in the collection. Select can also be used by any object as a whole. Our next example demonstrates the basic use of the Select query. Have a look at it:

Example4:

```
using System;
using System.Collections;
using System.Collections.Generic;
using System.Linq;
namespace MyCSharpApplication
{

    public class Person
    {

        public int age;
        public string name;

        public Person(int age, string name)
        {
            this.age = age;
            this.name = name;
        }

    }

    class Program
    {

        public static void Main()
        {
```

```
                Person p1 = new Person(9, "John");
                Person p2 = new Person(8, "Jack");
                Person p3 = new Person(13, "Mic");
                Person p4 = new Person(15, "Evens");
                Person p5 = new Person(6, "Roddy");

                List<Person> plist = new List<Person>();
                plist.Add(p1);
                plist.Add(p2);
                plist.Add(p3);
                plist.Add(p4);
                plist.Add(p5);

                List<string> personnames = plist.Where(p
=> p.age <= 10).Select(per => per.name).ToList();

                foreach(string pname in personnames)
                {
                        Console.WriteLine(pname);
                }

                Console.Read();
            }
        }
}
```

In Example4, we created a Person class with two member variables: age and name. These variables can be initialized via a constructor. Inside the main method of the program class, we created 5 objects of the Person class and then stored them in the Person list collection named plist. We then executed a LINQ query having the where and select operators. The where operator is used to filter all the persons whose age is less than 10. If we do not use a select operator here, the whole Person object will be retrieved. However, we are only interested in retrieving the names of the persons with an age less than 10. Therefore, we used the Select operator and passed it a Lambda Expression which selects the person name.

LINQ is a very vast subject, and requires a complete book in itself. We will end the discussion of the operators here. In the next two chapters, I will explain the process of connecting LINQ to SQL as well as connecting LINQ to XML.

Exercise 17

Task:

There exists a Car class with the following structure:

```
public class Car
{

    public int price;
    public string name;

    public Car(int cprice, string cname)
    {
        this.price = cprice;
        this.name = cname;
    }

}
```

In the Main method, 5 objects of the Car class have been initialized and stored in a List collection. This is shown below:

```
Car c1 = new Car(120000, "Honda");
```

```
            Car c2 = new Car(90000, "Toyota");
            Car c3 = new Car(130000, "BMW");
            Car c4 = new Car(150000, "Ferrari");
            Car c5 = new Car(30000, "Suzuki");

            List<Car> clist = new List<Car>();
            clist.Add(c1);
            clist.Add(c2);
            clist.Add(c3);
            clist.Add(c4);
            clist.Add(c5);
```

Your task is to Select names of all the cars where the price of the car is greater than or equal to 125,000.

Solution:

```
        List<string> carnames = clist.Where(c =>
c.price >= 125000).Select(car => car.name).ToList();

        foreach(string cname in carnames)
        {
            Console.WriteLine(cname);
        }
```

Chapter 18: LINQ part 2

What gives LINQ an edge over other technologies is its flexibility to work with multiple types of data. That is, with LINQ, the same query syntax can be used to handle incoming data, independent of the data source type, whereas all other technologies require writing separate queries for each source. SQL queries are required for interaction with the SQL server and Xquery for the XML data type.

In this chapter, we will see the relationship between:

Contents

- **LINQ and SQL**
- **LINQ and Lambda Expressions**

i.   **LINQ and SQL:**

LINQ is a smart alternative for the old mode of accessing SQL data using SQL queries. The term "LINQ to SQL" is often used to describe the relationship through which we can access SQL databases using

LINQ. The first step to do that is to map our existing/target SQL database to LINQ.

a. Mapping LINQ to SQL:

Mapping LINQ to SQL refers to .Net recognizing our existing database as Objects (Classes). This is quite easy actually; open Visual Studio-> target project in solution explorer. Next, click Add->New Item. Select "Data" from the "Categories" options, and choose "LINQ to SQL Classes" from the Templates on the left. A ".dbml" file will result with a Graphic User Interface (GUI). This GUI has two parts, one that allows you to drag and drop tables to auto create classes from them and the other part where we can drop stored procedures. Select, drag and drop all essential tables and procedures as needed.

b. Selecting Data:

As soon as we create our ".dbml" file, a corresponding "DataContext" class file is created on its own by the .NET framework that does all the communication with databases. LINQ queries then use objects from these classes to work with databases. Let's see this from the example below:

Example 1:

```
public bool checkValidUser(string Name, string
passcode)
{
DBToysDataContext sampleDB = new DBToysDataContext();
var getter = from u in sampleDB.Users
                    where u.Username == Name
                    && u.Password == passcode
                    select u;
return Enumerable.Count(getter) > 0;
}
```

Before diving into the code, it's important to know that when we mapped our "DBToys.dbml" file, a "DBToysDataContext" class file was created automatically. In the code above, we passed two strings "Name" and "Passcode" to our function "checkValidUser" which validates a user entered a name and password against the table "Users" from the database Toys. In the first line inside the function, we instantiated an object "sampleDB" to access our Toys database using the "DBToysDataContext" class file. Visual studio treats "u" from the line "from u in sampleDB.Users" as an object of the "Users" class, referring to our "Users" table from the Toys database. Next, note that we are passing our incoming column/field values as an object of type "var." The Var data type refers to dynamic data. Whatever types of data our LINQ query supplies it can be stored in a variable "getter." Here we are only retrieving and saving the username and password from the "Users" table. Lastly, the function "Enumerable.Count" returns the total number of data rows returned by our LINQ query.

However, there's an alternate way to access the same data without using SQL like syntax in LINQ.

Example 2

```
public    bool    checkValidUser(string    Name,    string
passcode)
{
        DBToysDataContext        sampleDB        =        new
DBToysDataContext();
        List<Users> getter = sampleDB.Users.Where(u =>
u.Username == Name && u.Password==passcode);
        if(users.Count>0)
        {
            return true;
```

```
        }
        return false;
}
```

Here, instead of using the traditional SQL syntax, we are using the "Where" method to directly access data from the "Users" table of the Toys database. The rest of the working process is the same as before, except here we have used the "List" data type to store the values returned from our LINQ query.

Example 3

```
    public User bringUser(string name)
{
    DBToysDataContext sampleDB = new
DBToysDataContext();
    User use = sampleDB.Users.Single(u,
u.UserName=>name);
    return use;
}
```

For cases where we only want to retrieve and send only a single row (object) using our LINQ query, we can easily do that as well. The function "bringUser" in its only argument accepts a name to be matched against objects in our "Users" table. The method "Single" in the line "sampleDB.Users.Single()" looks for a match against the provided name, and upon success returns only a single row(object) as required.

- **LINQ and Lambda Expressions**

While we have already discussed Lambda Expressions earlier, LINQ queries mostly imply Lambda Expressions in dealing with collections or lists of data to filter list items based on some specific criteria. Let's see how:

Example 4:

```
IEnumerable <SelectListItem> toys = database.Toys
        .Where(toy => toy.Tag == curTag.ID)
        .Select(toy => new SelectListItem { Value =
toy.Name, Text = toy.ID });

ViewBag.toySelector = toys;
```

In the code above, we have declared the variable "toys" and are casting it to type "SelectListItem" to save the resultant row from our LINQ query. We have used two methods, "Where" and "Select" to find the target toy that matches our query. The line "'toy => toy.Tag == curTag.ID" selects a toy based on a passed tag, whereas the line "toy => new SelectListItem {Value = toy.Name, Text = toy.ID" selects a particular toy based on a passed ID and name. The resultant toy that meets this criterion is saved in the "toys" variable.

Exercise 18

Task:

Using Customer table from DB NorthWind (Visual Studio), apply LINQ to insert/update and delete a customer where the ID is 20.

Solution:

```
namespace MySolutionApplication
```

```
{
        public static void InsertCustomer(string id,
string name, string city, string phone, string fax)
    {

        NorthWindDataClassesDataContext dco = new
        NorthWindDataClassesDataContext();

        var   lookCustomer   =   (   from   c   in
dc.GetTable<Customer>() where c.CustomerID == id
                     select c).SingleOrDefault();

        if(lookCustomer == null)
        {
            try
            {

                Table<Customer>            cus        =
Accessor.GetCustomerTable();
                Customer cust = new Customer();
                cust.CustomerID = id;
                cust.ContactName = name;
                cust.City = city;
                cust.Phone = phone;
                cust.Fax = fax;
                cus.InsertOnSubmit(cust);
                cus.Context.SubmitChanges();
            }
            catch (Exception ex)
            {
                throw ex;
            }
        }
        else
        {
            try
```

```
        {
            lookCustomer.ContactName = name;
            lookCustomer.City = city;
            lookCustomer.Phone = phone;
            lookCustomer.Fax = fax;

            dco.SubmitChanges();
        }
        catch (Exception ex)
        {
            throw ex;
        }
    }
}
public static void DeleteCustomer(string ID)
{
    NorthWindDataClassesDataContext dco = new
    NorthWindDataClassesDataContext();

    var    lookCustomer    =    (from    c    in
dc.GetTable<Customer>()    where c.CustomerID ==id
    select c).SingleOrDefault();

    try
    {

dco.Customers.DeleteOnSubmit(lookCustomer);
        dco.SubmitChanges();
    }
    catch (Exception ex)
    {
        throw ex;
    }
}
```

Chapter 19: LINQ part 3

In the previous chapter, we saw how we can use LINQ to work mainly with our SQL databases. In this chapter, however, we will see how we can use LINQ to work with XML data. XML, Extensible Markup Language, is used extensively on the World Wide Web and is much more than just a set of static text based labels. Also called self-describing and self-defining data, XML with its highly standardized and equally customizable tag usage is globally employed in sharing, accessing, and manipulating data.

Hence, in this chapter, we will see how we can use LINQ to:

Contents

- **Retrieve and delete XML data**
- **Insert and update XML data**

i. **Retrieve and delete XML data**

All XML data files have a root/parent tag (element) that not only encapsulates and defines the type of child records, but also defines their attributes. The subsequent child records (elements) contain actual data that we can manipulate as per our needs. Look at this sample XML code that we are using during rest of this chapter for dealing with LINQ queries.

Sample XML Data

```xml
<? Xml version='1.0' encoding='utf-8'?>
<Toys>
  <Toy ID='1'>
    <Name>Barbie</Name>
    <Price>$0.45</Price>
  </Toy>
  <Toy ID='2'>
    <Name>Pigeon</Name>
    <Price>$0.40</Price>
  </Toy>
  <Toy ID='3'>
    <Name>Crow</Name>
    <Price>$0.55</Price>
  </Toy>
</Toys>
```

Here "Toys" is our root element with multiple child "Toy" elements. Each child toy has an "ID" attribute with "Price" and "Name" inner elements.

Now, let's see how we can retrieve child toys from this XML data using LINQ queries.

Example 1

```
private string file = 'SampleData.xml';
```

```
private void GetData()
{
    try
    {
        XDocument doc = XDocument.Load(file);
        var  comingToys  =  from  toy  in
doc.Descendants('Toy')
        select new
        {
    ID= Convert.ToInt32(toy.Attribute('ID').Value),
    Name = toy.Element('Name').Value ,
Price = toy.Element('Price').Value
                                };

        foreach (var x in toys)
        {
    Console.WriteLine('Toy ID', x[ID]);
Console.WriteLine('Toy Name', x[Name]);
Console.WriteLine('Toy        Price',        x[Price]);
        }
    }
    catch (Exception err)
    {
        MessageBox.Show(err.Message);
    }
}
```

The first line here points to our sample XML data file "SampleData.xml". Inside the function, we first load our xml file using 'Load (file)' function. After loading our target file, we retrieve subsequent child "toy" elements using "Doc.descendants()" function. Next we select each child "toy" and retrieve each toy's ID attribute as well as its inner elements and pass them onto our dynamic variable "comingToys". The foreach" loop at the end then displays all the retrieved data.

Output 1:

```
Toy ID 1 Toy Name Barbie Toy Price $0.45
Toy ID 1 Toy Name Pigeon Toy Price $0.40
Toy ID 1 Toy Name Crow Toy Price $0.55
```

Similarly, if let's say we want to remove a child element from our sample XML data file, we can do that like this.

Example 2

```
private string file = 'SampleData.xml';

Private void DeleteData (int id)
        {
            try
            {
                XDocument           sampleXML        =
XDocument.Load(file);
                XElement            cToy             =
sampleXML.Descendants('Toy').Where(c           =>
c.Attribute('ID').Value.Equals(id);
                cToy.Remove();
                sampleXML.Save(file);
            }
            catch (Exception e)
            {
                MessageBox.Show(e.Message);
            }
        }
```

The code here, after loading the target file, traverses the child toys and looks for a match against the passed in "toy ID". Once it finds that child, it removes that child by calling the "Remove()" function and saves the resulting file.

ii. Insert and Update XML data:

Inserting data into existing XML files is not much different from retrieving data from the same file. Essentially, we will need an object of the type "XElement" with the same signature as our existing child/elements in the target XML file. The next step involves inserting that "XElement" object into our data file using an "XDocument" object.

Example 3

```
private string file = 'SampleData.xml';

private void InsertData(string name, string price)
        {
            try
            {
  XDocument doc = XDocument.Load(file);
            XElement newToy = new XElement('Toy', new
XElement('Name',    name),    new    XElement('Price',
price));
    Var lastToy = doc.Descendants('Toy').Last();
    Int    newID   = Convert.ToInt32   (lastToy.Attribute
('ID').Value);
    newToy.SetAttributeValue('ID',++newID);
        doc.Element ('Toys').Add (newToy);
            doc.Save (file);
                }
            catch (Exception err)
            {
                MessageBox.Show (err.Message);
            }
        }
```

After creating an object of the type "XDocument", we have created an "XElement" type object with same signature as our existing "Toy" elements in the line "XElement newToy = new XElement('Toy", new XElement('Name', name), new XElement('Price', price)'". Next, we get the last toy element in var lastToy using the "doc.Descendants('Toy').Last()" function. Once we have that, we get its "ID" value and then increment it while setting that attribute to our new toy element in line "newToy.SetAttributeValue('ID',++newID)". Finally, we insert our "toy" object using the "Add()" function, and then save our changes to the XML file.

Output 3:

Our sample XML data file will now contain a fourth child. In the file, it will look like this if, for instance, we had passed "Rabbit" as the name and "$0.65" as the price to the above function.

```
<Toy ID='4'>
   <Name>Rabbit</Name>
   <Price>$0.65</Price>
</Toy>
```

In order to make changes to existing data or elements in our XML file, we first need to locate our target element against some specific criteria whose data values we would like to alter. The line "XElement cToy = doc.Descendants('Toy').Where (c=>c.Attribute('ID').Value.Equals(id)" does exactly that for us. It looks for a match against our provided "id" and allows our "XElement" object "cToy" to point to that element. Once we have a reference to that element, we can easily update its inner elements values using "cToy.Element('Price').Value = price". Lastly, we need to save our XML file ("XDocument" object) to reflect these changes.

Example 4

```
private string file = 'SampleData.xml';
private void UpdateData(string name, string price,
int id)
        {
            try
            {
    XDocument doc = XDocument.Load(file);
    XElement    cToy    =    doc.Descendants('Toy').Where
(c=>c.Attribute('ID').Value.Equals(id);
 cToy.Element('Name').Value = name;
 cToy.Element('Price').Value = price;
        doc.Save(file);
            }
            catch (Exception err)
            {
                MessageBox.Show(err.Message);
            }
        }
```

Output 4:

Let's say that we have passed these values as arguments to our function above: id=1, name=Crocodile, price=$0.75. After executing the above function, our sample XML data file will no longer have the toy name=Barbie at id=1. Instead it will have a toy name=crocodile in its place.

```
<Toy ID='1'>
    <Name>Crocodile</Name>
    <Price>$0.75</Price>
</Toy>
```

Exercises 19

Task:

From the given XML sample data, use LINQ to create an XML file with the same data values.

XML Data:

```xml
<?xml version='1.0' encoding='utf-8' ?>
<Students>
    <student id='1' regular='no'>
        <name>Alberto Gustavo</name>
        <adm_date>7/31/1996</adm_date>
    </student>
    <student id='3' regular='yes'>
        <name>Kim Kards</name>
        <adm_date>12/12/1997</adm_date>
    </ student >
    < student id='8' regular='no'>
        <name>Carl Mills</name>
        < adm _date>2/6/1998</ adm _date>
    </ student >
    < student id='9' regular='yes'>
        <name>Adams</name>
        <adm_date>2/6/1998</ adm _date>
    </ student >
</Students >
```

Solution:

```
public static void CreateStudents()
{
    XDocument doc = new XDocument(
        new XDeclaration('1.0', 'utf-8', 'yes'),
```

175

```
        new XComment('Solution XML file'),
        new XElement('Students',
            new XElement('student',
                new XAttribute('id', 1),
                new XAttribute('regular', 'false'),
                    new    XElement('name',    '    Alberto
Gustavo'),
                new                    XElement('adm_date',
'7/31/1996')),
            new XElement('student',
                new XAttribute('id', 3),
                new XAttribute('regular', 'true'),
                    new XElement('name', 'Kim Kards'),
                new                    XElement('adm_date',
'12/12/1997')),
            new XElement('student',
                new XAttribute('id', 8),
                new XAttribute('regular', 'false'),
                    new XElement('name', 'Carl Mills'),
                    new XElement('adm_date', '2/6/1998')),
            new XElement('student',
                new XAttribute('id', 9),
                new XAttribute('regular', 'false'),
                    new XElement('name', 'Adams'),
                    new XElement('adm_date', '2/6/1998'))
        )
    );
}
```

Chapter 20: Asynchronous Programming

In this chapter, we are going to study a new feature of C# 5.0 that allows you to write your own asynchronous code. Imagine that you are working on a Windows form application, and you click a button to download an image from the web synchronously. It would take more than 30 seconds to download the image, and during this time your application becomes unresponsive, which from a usability perspective isn't a good thing. Hence, a better way to allow the downloading of the image is to do so asynchronously.

In this chapter, we will understand what "asynchronously" means in C#, and how we can use this feature in our applications.

Contents

- **Asynchronous Programming using async and await**

The problem we discussed above can be easily avoided using two keywords **"async"** and **"await"** in our programs. Let's discuss each of two now:

i. **Async**

    If we specify this keyword before a function while declaring it, it becomes an asynchronous function. By using this keyword, you can use the resources provided by the .NET framework to create an asynchronous framework, and the function will be called asynchronously. The syntax of asynchronous methods is like this:

```
public async void MyProcess()
        { }
```

The above declared function is ready to be called asynchronously.

ii. **Await**

    While the "Async" keyword is used to tell the compiler that the function is asynchronous, the function also needs to have "await" in it. The syntax of await is as follows:

```
public async void MyProcess()
{
// do the asynchronous work
 await Task.delay(5);
}
```

The above mentioned method will do the work after a delay of 5 seconds.

Let's talk about the problem stated at the beginning of the chapter. The following lines of C# code will download the image from the web synchronously.

Example 1

```
 private void button_Click(object sender, EventArgs
e)
{
    WebClient image = new WebClient();
    byte[] imageData =
image.DownloadData('http://urlOfTheImage');
    this.imageView.Image = Image.FromStream(new
MemoryStream(imageData));
}
```

Your application will become unresponsive during the execution of this code. While on the other hand, we can easily do it using new keywords provided by C# 5.0 async and await. Let's see how:

Example 2

```
private   async   void   button_Click(object   sender,
EventArgs e)
{
    WebClient image = new WebClient();
    byte[]           imageData          =           await
image.DownloadDataTaskAsync('http://urlOfTheImage');
    this.imageView.Image    =    Image.FromStream(new
MemoryStream(imageData));
}
```

The above mentioned code looks identical to the one in Example 1, but it is not. There are three differences:

- The addition of the async keyword in the method.
- The call to download the image from the web is preceded by await.

- DownloadData is replaced by its asynchronous counterpart DownloadDataTaskAsync.

The "DownloadData" method of the WebClient class downloads the data synchronously and then after downloading returns the control to the caller which causes the application to become unresponsive. On the other hand, "DownloadDataTaskAsync" returns immediately and downloads the data asynchronously. The await keyword is the most interesting part as it releases the UI thread unless the download is complete. Whenever the code encounters the await keyword, the function returns, and when the specified operation completes, the function resumes. It continues executing from where it has stopped.

NOTE: Every asynchronous method can return three types of values.

- Void: return nothing.
- Task: It will perform one operation.
- Task<T>: Will return a task with a T type parameter.

Task: A Task returns no value (it is void). A Task<int> returns an element of the type int. This is a generic type.

Note: An async method will run synchronously if it does not contain the await keyword.

Example 3:

```
using System;
using System.IO;
using System.Threading.Tasks;

class Program
{
    static void Main()
```

180

```csharp
    {
        Task task = new Task(ProcessDataAsync);
        task.Start();
        task.Wait();
        Console.ReadLine();
    }

    static async void ProcessDataAsync()
    {

        Task<int>                task                =
HandleFileAsync('C:\\enable1.txt');


        Console.WriteLine('Please wait patiently ' +
            'while I do something important.');


        int x = await task;
        Console.WriteLine('Count: ' + x);
    }

    static async Task<int> HandleFileAsync(string
file)
    {
        Console.WriteLine('HandleFile enter');
        int count = 0;


        using (StreamReader reader = new
StreamReader(file))
        {
            string v = await reader.ReadToEndAsync();
```

```
                count += v.Length;


        for (int i = 0; i < 10000; i++)
        {
            int x = v.GetHashCode();
            if (x == 0)
            {
                count--;
            }
        }
    }
    Console.WriteLine('HandleFile exit');
    return count;
    }
}
```

Output initial 3:

```
HandleFile enter
Please wait patiently while I do something important.
```

Output final 3:

```
HandleFile enter
Please wait patiently while I do something important.
HandleFile exit
Count: 1916146
```

In the above example, after the main method we create an instance of Task with the ProcessDataAsync method passed as an argument. Then in the next line we start this task with "task.Start()" and then wait for it to finish with the "task.Wait()" method. The method "ProcessDataAsync" is an asynchronous method as the "async" in the method signature tells us. Hence the keyword await is mandatory here. The first line inside method, "Task<int> task = HandleFileAsync('C:\\enable1.txt')" calls another method "HandleFileAsync". As this is an asynchronous method, control returns here before the "HandleFileAsync" method returns as we discussed in the above example. Meanwhile as "HandleFileAsync" method is performing its task we display a message on the screen "HandleFile enter" & "Please wait patiently while I do something important." Here, the first line is from the method "HandleFileAsync." This happens because when the method is called, it is gets printed to the screen and then control returns back to the method "ProcessDataAsync". Next the second line is printed to the screen. Now the next line "await task" of the method "ProcessDataAsync" tells it to wait for the HandleFile task to complete, and then assigns the total computed result to the variable "x" and finally prints it on the screen.

Now let's talk about the next method "HandleFileAsync," which is also an asynchronous method as the async in the method signature tells us, and hence has an await keyword as well. After the first line prints on the screen, we initialize a dummy integer variable "count" and set it equal to "0" as we passed the location of a file in the argument when we call this method which is "C:\\enable1.txt". Now in order to read the data from this file, we initialize a reader of the type "StreamReader" and pass it the location of our file. To read this file, we use the asynchronous built-in method "reader.ReadToEndAsync();" and tell it to wait until it finishes reading the file with the "await" keyword. Then we assign the result to a string type variable "v". Finally, we add the total length of the string to the dummy variable "count". Then we put in some dummy code to count this value. This dummy code is just for your understanding, and at the end when this method returns, a simple line "HandleFile exit" prints on the screen. The dummy value also gets printed.

Exercise 20

Task:

Write code for a Windows application which creates an asynchronous function that will wait for two minutes.

Solution

```
using System;
using System.ComponentModel;
using System.Threading.Tasks;
using System.Windows.Forms;

namespace WindowsFormsApplication
{
    public partial class Form2 : Form
    {
        public Form2()
        {
            InitializeComponent();
        }

        public static Task awaitedProcess()
        {
            return Task.Run(() =>
            {
                System.Threading.Thread.Sleep(2000);
            });
        }

        public async void myProcess ()
        {
            await awaitedProcess();
            this.listBox.Items.Add('Awaited    Process
finish');
```

```
        }

        private void Form2_Load(object sender, EventA
rgs e)
        {
        }

        private async void button1_Click(object sende
r, EventArgs e)
        {
            myProcess();
            this.listBox.Items.Add('Process
finish');
        }
    }
}
```

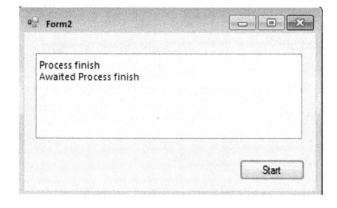

Other Books by the Author

Java Programming

http://www.linuxtrainingacademy.com/java-programming

Java is one of the most widely used and powerful computer programming languages in existence today. Once you learn how to program in Java you can create software applications that run on servers, desktop computers, tablets, phones, Blu-ray players, and more.

Also, if you want to ensure your software behaves the same regardless of which operation system it runs on, then Java's "write once, run anywhere" philosophy is for you. Java was design to be platform independent allowing you to create applications that run on a variety of operating systems including Windows, Mac, Solaris, and Linux.

JavaScript: A Guide to Learning the JavaScript Programming Language
http://www.linuxtrainingacademy.com/javascript

JavaScript is a dynamic computer programming language that is commonly used in web browsers to control the behavior of web pages and interact with users. It allows for asynchronous communication and can update parts of a web page or even replace the entire content of a web page. You'll see JavaScript being used to display date and time information, perform animations on a web site, validate form input, suggest results as a user types into a search box, and more.

PHP
http://www.linuxtrainingacademy.com/php-book

PHP is one of the most widely used open source, server side programming languages. If you are interested in getting started with programming and want to get some basic knowledge of the language, then this book is for you! Popular websites such as Facebook and Yahoo are powered by PHP. It is, in a sense, the language of the web.

The book covers core PHP concepts, starting from the basics and moving into advanced object oriented PHP. It explains and demonstrates everything along the way. You'll be sure to be programming in PHP in no time.

Scrum Essentials: Agile Software Development and Agile Project Management for Project Managers, Scrum Masters, Product

Owners, and Stakeholders
http://www.linuxtrainingacademy.com/scrum-book

You have a limited amount of time to create software, especially when you're given a deadline, self-imposed or not. You'll want to make sure that the software you build is at least decent but more importantly, on time. How do you balance quality with time? This book dives into these very important topics and more.

www.ingramcontent.com/pod-product-compliance
Lightning Source LLC
Chambersburg PA
CBHW070946050326
40689CB00014B/3369